Living Beyond Brain Injury

A resource manual

DR VICKI HALL

Consultant Clinical Neuropsychologist
Neuromindworks Ltd, Sutton Coldfield, UK

Foreword by
PROFESSOR NARINDER KAPUR

Consultant Clinical Neuropsychologist
University College London, London, UK
Imperial College Healthcare NHS Trust, London, UK

First published in 2014 by
Speechmark Publishing Ltd, St Mark's House, Shepherdess Walk,
London N1 7BQ, UK
Tel: +44 (0)20 7954 3400

www.speechmark.net

002-5988/Printed in the United Kingdom by CMP (uk) Ltd
Designed and typeset by Darkriver Design, Auckland, New Zealand
British Library Cataloguing-in-Publication Data
A catalogue record for this book is available from the British Library

ISBN 978 190930 142 9

Contents

Foreword

Brain injury rehabilitation has gained prominence in recent years, in terms of its profile in the media, in terms of organisations that have been formed to cater for this field, and in terms of research that has been carried out. Most important, there has also in recent times been an increased awareness and higher expectations of brain-injured patients and their families with regard to the services that they should receive. This in an era where there is a greater realisation that resources for healthcare are limited and that patients and their families may often have to fend for themselves with regard to certain aspects of their care.

In this context, a book such as this one by Dr Vicki Hall is to be welcomed. She has set out clearly and concisely, and in language that patients and their families can readily understand, how to cope with cognitive, emotional and behavioural changes that come about following a serious brain injury or illness. She also deals with those factors such as fatigue and sleep that may affect cognition and emotion, and she covers important areas of readjustment in the community, such as going back to work and driving. In addition to providing an excellent overview of these various domains, Dr Hall has helpfully provided a series of appendices that offer a set of practical guidelines to help implement therapeutic activities.

Brain injury patients and their families will find such a resource invaluable, as will practitioners in the field.

Professor Narinder Kapur
Consultant Clinical Neuropsychologist
March 2014

About the author

Dr Vicki Hall is a consultant clinical neuropsychologist and a chartered clinical psychologist. She is on the British Psychological Society's Specialist Register in Clinical Neuropsychology and is registered as a clinical psychologist by the Health and Care Professions Council. She is director of Neuromindworks Ltd. This is an independent practice providing neuropsychological assessments and interventions for private patients, private organisations and legal and insurance firms. She provides community, inpatient and residential neuropsychology services.

Dr Hall has worked in clinical psychology and neuropsychology settings for over 10 years, and has worked across a range of neurological services spanning the whole care pathway (eg surgery, outpatient diagnostic services, inpatient and community rehabilitation services).

She has published numerous articles in the area of neuropsychology and acts as an ad hoc peer reviewer for a number of academic journals. She is a lecturer on the Staffordshire University Clinical Psychology Professional Doctorate programme and was employed as an associate lecturer at the clinical neuropsychology MSc and postgraduate diploma course at The University of Nottingham. Dr Hall has made numerous presentations in the field of neuropsychology at both national and international levels.

Acknowledgements

This book started as a series of self-help leaflets and exercises to help my clients within the context of my clinical practice. I would like to thank Drs Andrew Worthington, Jamie Macniven and Dene Fokias for looking over early drafts of the leaflets.

I would particularly like to thank all my clients whose experiences helped to shape this book and my clinical practice. A special thanks goes to those clients who have let me use examples of their experiences to illustrate this book.

Introduction

A 'brain injury' refers to damage to the brain that was sudden in onset and which occurred after birth. Damage to the brain may be caused by:

- trauma, injuries sustained by a blow to the head or as a result of surgery (eg following a tumour removal)
- a stroke, which is caused by a disturbance in blood supply to the brain occurring because of a restriction in the blood supply (eg ischaemia) or a leakage of blood (eg haemorrhage)
- a lack of oxygen to the brain (cerebral anoxia), caused by a heart attack, surgery or substance misuse
- other toxic or metabolic insult (eg hypoglycaemic attack associated with diabetes)
- infection (eg meningitis, encephalitis).

A brain injury can have a dramatic effect on all areas of a person's life. This manual is designed to provide an understanding of some of the effects of a brain injury and how to manage them. It focuses on how brain injury may affect thinking skills (eg memory), emotions and other related areas (eg fatigue and sleep). It is a resource that may be useful for brain injury survivors, their loved ones and brain injury professionals. It has particular use as a self-help resource for clinicians to work through with brain injury survivors. The techniques illustrated in this manual are not a substitute for seeing a clinical psychologist or a doctor.

Users are referred to the enclosed CD for printable versions of the worksheets and templates.

Part 1

Understanding and management

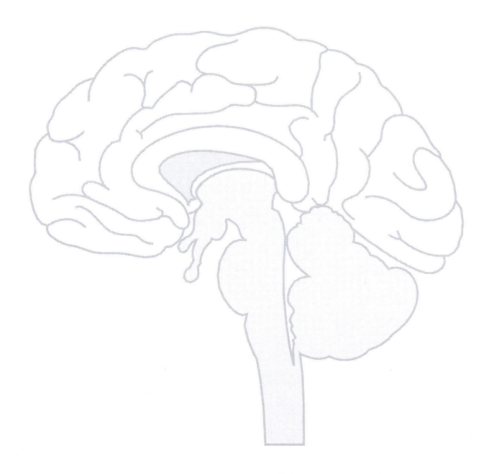

Chapter 1

Understanding and managing
low mood

Why is low mood common following a brain injury?

It is common to experience low mood following a brain injury. This is because people who have had a brain injury may experience a number of losses (eg loss of previous ability to remember things, loss of physical abilities, loss of independence, loss of social activities), which can affect relationships and social roles (eg role as an employee, mother or father) and reduce confidence to cope in everyday life. It is natural to go through a grieving process for these losses and to experience feelings such as low mood, anger and frustration.

Over time, people who have had a brain injury tend to gradually regain some of their lost abilities and learn to adapt to their problems. Most improvements are seen in the first six months to a year following the injury, with the natural recovery of the brain tending to stop after two years. Adapting to problems may include having to make lifestyle changes or changing plans and hopes for the future. Low mood often fades as improvements are made, but this does not always happen and people can become stuck in a grieving process, leading to depression.

How do I know if I am depressed?

Depression is indicated by consistent feelings of depressed mood (most of the day, nearly every day) that last for longer than two weeks. Other signs of depression include:

- having no interest in things you used to enjoy
- regular feelings of worthlessness, hopelessness or guilt
- having no energy or motivation
- a change in appetite
- sad thoughts
- sleeping significantly more or less than usual
- crying.

Depression can be more difficult to diagnose in brain injury because some of these symptoms may be caused by other factors and do not necessarily mean you are depressed. Some examples are as follows.

- Poor motivation may be due to damage to the brain that has affected your ability to kick-start yourself into action (*see* Chapter 10, 'Understanding and managing executive skills').
- Poor sleep may be due to a range of factors associated with your brain injury (*see* Chapter 6, 'Understanding and managing sleep problems').
- You may have lost interest in the things you used to enjoy because you are no longer capable of doing them because of changes in your thinking skills or physical problems.
- Crying can sometimes be due to 'emotionalism' (*see* Chapter 2, 'Understanding and managing emotionalism').

In brain injury, the most important symptoms to look for are feelings of depressed mood in addition to sad thoughts (eg guilty thoughts or thoughts about being worthless, helpless or things being hopeless). Depression can be treated, and it is important to manage depression by asking for help from your general practitioner, who can refer you to a psychologist as soon as possible and/or provide any necessary medication.

How can I improve my mood?

Often people feel depressed because they experience a number of difficulties following a brain injury (eg fatigue, poor memory). If you can understand these problems and find ways to manage them this will help to improve your mood. Many ways to understand these problems and improve your mood are discussed further on in this book (eg *see* Chapter 5, 'Understanding and managing fatigue').

Having difficulty accepting or adapting to problems can sometimes cause depression. Some people are more prone to not accepting difficulties than others, as each person has an individual coping style developed prior to their brain injury (*see* 'How can I manage my perfectionism?' in Chapter 4, 'Understanding and managing anxiety', p18). A person may also feel they are not progressing and feel hopeless about getting their life back on track and heading in a desired direction. It can therefore be useful to set goals and to monitor goal progress (*see* Appendix 1, 'Goal-setting').

Depression can also be partly maintained and caused by low activity levels. This is because the more depressed you feel, the more you will feel like giving up and doing less. If you have low activity levels, you will stop doing things that you enjoy, you will not learn to adapt to your problems and you will be unlikely to notice any improvements. It will also mean that you have little in your life to give you a sense of value and worth, which can maintain feelings of hopelessness (*see* Figure 1).

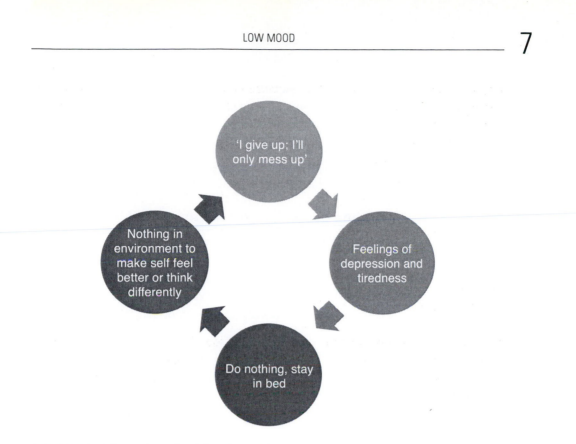

FIGURE 1 Activity cycle maintaining depression

To escape the negative cycle of depression, therefore, it can help to increase your activity levels and set yourself goals that give you a sense of mastery and pleasure (*see* Appendix 2, 'Guidelines for increasing the number of pleasurable activities').

What psychological barriers may stop me moving forwards, and how can I overcome them?

It can sometimes be difficult to motivate yourself to attempt goals, particularly if you are depressed, and often people will put things off, or 'procrastinate'. This tendency can be overcome by providing yourself with motivational statements and reviewing the pros and cons of delaying doing something (*see* Appendix 3, 'Guidelines for procrastinating').

Goal-setting may also be delayed because of a fear of failure or a fear of not getting things exactly right (*see* 'How can I manage my perfectionism?' in Chapter 4, 'Understanding and managing anxiety', p18, and Appendix 10, 'Guidelines for dealing with perfectionism'). In these cases, it may sometimes help to set goals that do not revolve around doing things to the best possible standard (eg cooking a meal without making any mistakes). Instead, it may help to focus on accepting your problems and being content with yourself and your achievements in the here and now rather than always needing to search or wait for something to happen in the future to make you feel content (*see* Appendix 12 for an acceptance exercise, and 'Mindfulness exercises' in Appendix 5, 'Guidelines for mindfulness', on p64).

There may also be a number of other barriers that prevent you moving forwards, such as fatigue, pain and other anxieties, which are discussed in later chapters of this book.

How can I overcome gloomy thoughts?

When people are depressed, they start to view the world through 'gloomy glasses', which filter in and magnify negative experiences. While they are wearing these glasses, they are only likely to pay attention to information that confirms their negative thoughts about themselves, the world and others. When depressed, it is therefore important to try to help yourself think more objectively about things. You may be able to do this by:

- recognising that you are looking though the gloomy glasses again
- using thought-challenging techniques (*see* Appendix 4, 'Guidelines for thought-challenging')
- trying not to worry about the future or past; learn to focus on the here and now (*see* 'Mindfulness exercises' in Appendix 5, 'Guidelines for mindfulness', p64).

Chapter 2

Understanding and managing
emotionalism

What is 'emotionalism'?

After people have had a brain injury, they sometimes find that they overreact by laughing or crying uncontrollably in a way that seems out of proportion to the situation. The person's actual feelings at this time may not match his or her behaviour (eg the person may cry hysterically but only feel moderately sad). Signs of emotionalism include:

- sudden and brief episodes of laughing or crying that:
  - may occur without an environmental cause or be excessive responses to the cause
  - feel uncontrollable
  - may not mirror your internal emotions.
- your emotions being very close to the surface, with small things causing you to be emotional (eg you might get upset more easily or cry at things you would never have cried at before)
- sudden swings from laughing to crying.

This condition is usually called 'emotionalism', but other terms used to refer to it include 'emotional lability', 'pathological laughing and/or crying' and 'pseudo-bulbar affect'. These reactions occur mostly in the first weeks after a brain injury and are likely to ease over time.

What causes emotionalism?

It is thought that emotionalism is caused when damage occurs to the parts of the brain that have control of the motor patterns involved in laughing and crying. Emotionalism is not thought to be caused by depression, but it can also occur alongside it.

Emotionalism can often cause anxiety and distress because people may worry about what others think of them; they may have fears of losing control or think that it is a sign that they are acutely distressed. This distress can make the symptoms worse. If the individual is not concerned about these episodes, they are harmless; the episodes are *not* an indication that the person is depressed or losing control.

How can I help myself?

- Try to distract yourself by thinking of enjoyable things or describing an object in detail.
- Focus on your feelings in the here and now, and tell yourself that the episode will soon pass.
- Use mindfulness exercises or relaxation techniques (*see* Appendix 5, 'Guidelines for mindfulness', and Appendix 6, 'Guidelines for relaxation', respectively).

How can other people help?

- If your symptoms persist, antidepressants may be prescribed by a doctor.
- Often family members may find these episodes difficult to deal with, as they may think your uncontrollable crying episodes are a sign that you are acutely distressed or depressed. It may be useful to let people know why you are acting the way you are. If you find it difficult to explain, you could provide them with a copy of the information written in this chapter.
- Let family members and friends know how you would like them to react or behave when you have an episode of emotionalism. It sometimes helps if they do not respond as though you are acutely distressed and instead encourage you to continue a normal conversation and not dwell on the episode. If it helps, you can also ask someone else to distract you or change the topic.
- Being told not to cry is sometimes not helpful, as it will not help to stop your tears, and it may cause you to become more frustrated.
- Tell people if you are genuinely upset, so they do not confuse it with emotionalism. This may help them to continue to show you empathy when you need it.

Chapter 3

Understanding and managing
anger and irritability

Why do I feel more angry?

It is common to experience increases in feelings of frustration and anger following a brain injury. This can be because you have a number of new problems to deal with (eg forgetfulness, feeling tired and being in pain), which may result in growing frustrations and being quick to anger, sometimes referred to as having a 'short fuse'. A good way to look at your capacity to cope with frustrating situations is the 'leaky bucket analogy'. If you do not experience any frustrating problems throughout the day, your capacity (the bucket) to handle frustrating situations is at its highest. However, if you experience many frustrating problems throughout the day, you will have a low threshold for dealing with frustration (ie your frustrations will gradually fill the bucket up so that something fairly minor may cause your frustrations to spill over, resulting in feelings

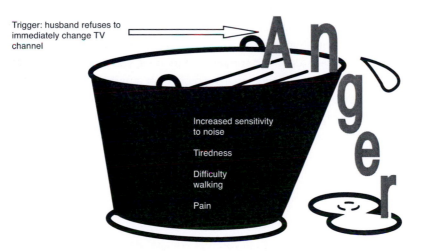

FIGURE 2 Leaky bucket of frustrations
Source: adapted from Davies W, 2000, *Overcoming Anger and Irritability*, Constable & Robinson, London.

 11

of anger). If you take time out from your problems, the frustrations will gradually drain from the bucket, and your frustration tolerance will return to full capacity.

Why do I find it more difficult to stop myself from venting my anger?

It is not uncommon for individuals to become aggressive (as evidenced, for example, by shouting or throwing things) following a brain injury, even if they were mild natured before. This anger may feel sudden and excessive. This is sometimes because the part of the brain responsible for your ability to control your impulses and think before you act has been affected. As your anger builds up, the more difficult it is to 'put the brakes on' and stop yourself from becoming aggressive or doing something you might later regret. It is likely there will be particular signs that indicate you are going to become angry, and it is important to recognise these early warning signs, so that you can curtail your feelings before they become unmanageable. Some early signs of anger are:

- raised voice
- muscle tension
- quicker breathing
- faster heartbeat
- higher temperature.

What can I do to control angry feelings?

1. Recognise and manage triggers to anger

Record any times when you feel angry and any direct triggers (ie what it was that caused you to become angry at that moment in time) in an anger diary (*see* Appendix 7, 'Anger'). Once you have identified some of the triggers, you may be able to avoid them (eg if you hate your partner watching a soap on TV at a particular time of day, you can plan to do something else then). Also note any problems you experience throughout the day that are likely to reduce your frustration tolerance (indirect triggers that fill up your 'leaky bucket' [*see* p11]). If you identify these problems, you may be able to find ways to manage them (*see*, for example, Chapter 5, 'Understanding and managing fatigue', and Chapter 7, 'Understanding and managing chronic pain') and to put into perspective the direct trigger that made you angry.

2. Nip angry feelings in the bud

Try to make a note of signs that tell you that you are starting to get angry (eg a racing heart). As mentioned in the previous section, these early warning signs may be an indication that you need to leave a situation before your anger builds and to help you stop yourself from doing something that you may later regret. When you are feeling

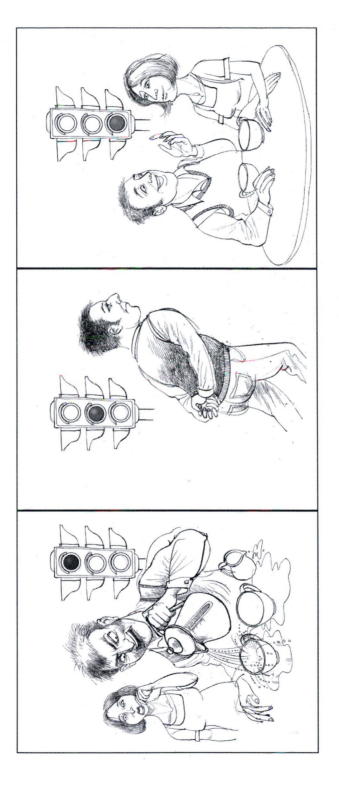

angry, it may be worthwhile to excuse yourself from others and say, 'I feel angry and need time out'.

A useful analogy for looking at your angry feelings is the traffic light system. The red light means that you are angry and you need to stop immediately; amber means that the early warning signs to your anger are building up, and you need to put your brakes on to either calm down or leave the situation; and green means you are not at all angry and it is OK to carry on doing whatever you want to.

Anger: emergency

Early warning signs to anger: put brakes on

Relaxed: go

FIGURE 3 Traffic light system for anger

3. Calm yourself down

● Use relaxation techniques (*see* Appendix 5, 'Guidelines for mindfulness').
● Challenge your angry thoughts: your angry thoughts will maintain feelings of anger. When we are caught up in angry feelings it is often difficult to view things from another perspective. Our thoughts can therefore sometimes be biased, so it can be useful to examine the evidence for and against our angry thoughts in a logical and structured way (*see* Appendix 4, 'Guidelines for thought-challenging', and Appendix 8, 'Coping with angry thoughts', for the application of these guidelines to anger).

4. Accept and manage what made you angry

If people make you angry, once your traffic light has changed back to green, you may want to explain to them what it was that made you angry and ask them why they did what they did so that you can understand them. It is better to do this once you have calmed down and thought about things – that is, without your 'angry head' on – by using thought-challenging guidelines (*see* Appendix 4).

Chapter 4

Understanding and managing **anxiety**

What fears are common after a brain injury?

Anxiety is a common symptom following a brain injury. Common fears include the following.

- That what caused the brain injury will happen again. This may result in thoughts such as: 'I may get knocked over by a car', 'I can't drive again because I am worried I will have another accident' and 'I can't go out because I will get attacked again'.
- Feeling worthless or stupid if you make a mistake when you try something new. This may result in thoughts such as: 'I'm too scared to speak to people in case I get my words muddled up', 'I'm worried about getting on the bus, in case I can't get the right change' and 'I'm too slow or I get stuck on what to say'.
- That other people will notice there is something wrong with you if you go out in public. This may result in thoughts such as: 'Other people will notice that I have scars and they won't want to be around me' and 'I can't handle the thought of people thinking that there is something wrong with me and feeling sorry for me; I'm not going out'.

Physical symptoms of anxiety include a pounding heart, rapid breathing, feeling dizzy, tense muscles, tingling feelings and a tight chest. They are part of the 'fight or flight response', which is the body's way of preparing you to fight or run away if you feel under threat. For example, if you are under attack, your muscles need to be tense and ready for action, your heart and breathing rates need to increase to allow blood and oxygen to go to your muscles so they can respond quickly and readily, and it is important to sweat to stop your body overheating. Although it might have been useful long ago when we lived in caves, this fight or flight response is not always helpful today.

Fear of social situations

After a brain injury, people often worry more about what others think of them (eg they may worry that others will think they are a fool if they make a mistake). This fear of negative evaluation is known as 'social anxiety'. It commonly causes people to avoid going out or facing others. This avoidance is an unhelpful strategy, as it will prevent you from becoming used to social situations and learning that you can cope with them and feel fine. You may only feel able to socialise if you use 'safety behaviours' that help reduce anxiety in the short term (eg only going out with your partner), but these are likely to maintain anxiety in the long run, as they will prevent you from realising you can cope without them.

How can I overcome this fear?

Try not to focus on yourself

Socially anxious people worry more about how they appear to others, which makes them focus more on themselves and pay less attention to how others are responding to them. This means that they do not pick up others' reactions to them (eg whether they are responding positively or negatively) and their beliefs about what other people think of them are based on assumptions, with little evidence to support them. It also means that they are not concentrating on the social situation, so they are more likely to make mistakes or miss social cues. This increases the likelihood of social mishaps and, consequently, exacerbates anxiety. Therefore, it is important to try to pay attention to the facial expressions of other people and what they are saying.

Face your fear

The best way to overcome your fear is to face it. You can do this gradually in a way that feels safe by using a technique called 'systematic desensitisation' (*see* Appendix 9, 'Fear-busting'). It is also important to become aware of what you do to prevent yourself from becoming anxious (eg avoiding eye contact, going out with only friends) as these are likely to be 'safety behaviours' and although they may reduce the anxiety in the short term, in the long term they will maintain it. Slowly try to reduce these safety behaviours.

Make a list of what you used to do and what you do now

Try to slowly get back to doing what you used to do. Again it is important to start with something relatively easy, and build up to something more difficult.

Challenge your anxious thoughts

● Often our fears are based on thoughts that may not have any basis in fact (eg 'Others think I am a fool'). It may therefore be useful to examine the evidence for and against your thoughts in a systematic way (a worksheet for this purpose is provided in Appendix 4, 'Guidelines for thought-challenging' – *see* Worksheet A4.1 on p63).

Fears about being knocked over

If you have a head injury caused by getting knocked over, it is understandable that you will worry about this happening again. Often people cope with this fear by avoiding (eg they do not go out or they avoid crossing the road), but the more you avoid similar situations, the harder it becomes to face them. To feel safe crossing the road or going out in public again, you need to gradually expose yourself to these situations.

How can I overcome this fear?

● Gradually expose yourself to going out, crossing the road again and doing the other things you previously did (*see* Appendix 9 for fear-busting techniques to help you gradually face your fear).

Fears about making mistakes or your disability being evident to others

Fear of making mistakes

It is not uncommon to worry about making mistakes following a brain injury. This is because you are more likely to make errors in simple tasks (eg cooking) because of problems with physical abilities and thinking skills. If you had very high standards for yourself and others (perfectionistic traits) prior to your injury, you are likely to be particularly hard on yourself because of your disability or impairments or if you make benign everyday mistakes. No one can be perfect, so if you are striving to achieve perfection, your standards are too high. Such unachievable goals are likely to make you feel anxious, particularly if you are critical of yourself for not achieving them.

How can having standards that are too high be problematic?

People may adopt the following strategies to cope with fears about making mistakes or the need to achieve '110 per cent'.

● They avoid trying things they consider difficult or, alternatively, they may become so frustrated about making mistakes that they give up. This is unhelpful because you can only improve if you try things that will stretch you, which will increase the likelihood of making a mistake.

● They avoid accepting that they make mistakes or find things difficult (eg by blaming others for their mistakes or simply denying that they have a problem). This is not useful because you need to be aware of your weaknesses so that you can compensate for or improve on them.

● They push themselves too hard, only attempt goals that are unrealistic or will not use strategies to help with their problems (eg because of physical problems, it may be easier for a person to attempt cooking sitting down, but they may only agree to cook standing up; a person may refuse to use alarm prompts to help them remember things because they think, 'I am not going to accept using a strategy that means I am less than perfect or have a disability'). As a result, they are likely to fail at achieving their goals or make mistakes, which can result in frustration and feelings of failure.

- They get so obsessed with achieving perfection that they work on the minute (small details), neglect the bigger picture and miss deadlines.
- They are never happy with the goals that they achieve, so they are never content with themselves in the here and now (eg an individual may not even be happy with winning a race, thinking he or she could have done it in a better time).

Worrying about making mistakes can also cause you to feel very anxious, and although moderate levels of anxiety are important to help improve your performance, too much anxiety is likely to make your performance worse. For example, if you were taking a driving test, a little anxiety would increase your adrenaline levels and keep you alert, but too much anxiety would make it hard to concentrate. Having very high expectations of yourself can thus actually increase the chances of making mistakes.

How can I manage my fear of making mistakes?

Do not be hard on yourself

After a brain injury, people can be very critical of themselves when they make a mistake, find something difficult or are not improving fast enough. It can sometimes be hard to be kind to yourself when this happens, but for a different perspective, think about what a friend may say in response to your critical voice (*see* Appendix 13, 'Compassionate mind exercise'). Also, be realistic and tell yourself that everyone makes errors.

Face your fear of making mistakes

You may need to face this gradually by attempting tasks of increasing levels of difficulty – that is, starting with something that you know is easy and gradually stretching yourself to attempt more difficult tasks.

Do not procrastinate

Often people put things off (ie procrastinate) if they are worried about not doing 'well enough' (*see* Appendix 3 for guidelines on how to manage procrastination).

Reframe perfectionism: 'When perfect is not good enough'

If you are a perfectionist, you are likely to have problems accepting your difficulties, and your drive to achieve 110 per cent is likely to impede your ability to adapt to and compensate for your problems. In this case, it may sometimes help to set goals that do not revolve around doing things to the best possible standard (eg cooking a meal without any mistakes) but instead focus on goal achievement on acceptance of problems, so that you can move forwards (*see* Appendix 12, 'Acceptance exercise').

Challenge the thoughts that make you anxious

Thoughts are often based on predictions that are unlikely to be true (eg 'Others will think I am a fool if I make mistakes'). Thus, it is important to examine the evidence for and against these thoughts (*see* Appendix 4, Worksheet A4.1 on p63).

Challenge the thoughts that make you think it is good to be a perfectionist

People often do not want to give up perfectionism because they have beliefs about why it is so important to have high standards and they have held these beliefs throughout their lives (eg 'If I do not achieve high standards, it means that I am not a worthwhile person' or 'Striving to achieve perfectionist standards has done nothing but make me achieve the best possible outcome for myself throughout my life'). As such, it can be useful to examine the evidence for and against the truth of these beliefs throughout your life (*see* Appendix 10, 'Guidelines for dealing with perfectionism').

Challenge beliefs that you were perfect before your brain injury and that you always make mistakes now

Sometimes people will set themselves standards that are higher than those they set themselves prior to their injury. This is because people often view how they were before the brain injury through rose-tinted glasses, remembering only the positive aspects of themselves (eg they think, 'I never made mistakes before my brain injury and my memory was 100 per cent perfect'), and see themselves through gloomy glasses after their brain injury (eg 'I always make mistakes now'). This is known as the 'good old days' bias.

● When people have this bias, they may have a tendency to attribute all mistakes (eg memory slips) to their brain injury and fail to recognise that they made mistakes before. This can cause people to be hard on themselves and make them think that they have more severe problems than they really have. It can be useful to challenge such beliefs (*see* Appendix 11, '"Good old days" bias exercise').

Chapter 5

Understanding and managing
fatigue

What is 'fatigue'?

After a brain injury, it is common to experience severe and persistent tiredness or drowsiness (fatigue). This tiredness may feel different to the general fatigue that you felt before your brain injury. For example, it may feel like a 'fog' clouding your mind or that you are running on a flat battery that makes you shut down and have an over-whelming need to sleep.

Fatigue can cause problems with sleeping, thinking skills (eg memory), motivation and mood. It can also make pre-existing problems worse (eg if you have problems walking or speaking, you may find these become worse when you are tired). In many cases, fatigue can be very disabling, making it difficult to perform everyday tasks such as household chores.

What can I do to manage my fatigue?

1. Recognise the signs of fatigue

Often people do not notice when they are getting tired. This is because they are so focused on getting through their day that they do not pay attention to the signs of fatigue. For example, a person running a marathon sometimes does not notice how exhausted he or she is until the end of the race. Ignoring the signs of fatigue is often not useful because, to manage fatigue, you need to pace yourself and recognise when you need to slow down or take a break (eg if you were running a marathon and sprinted from the beginning, you would soon run out of steam and would not be able to complete it). People may experience observable signs of tiredness that tell them they are becoming fatigued (eg slurred speech, heavy legs). It can sometimes help to become aware of and recognise these signs so that you are able to identify when you are getting tired and need to slow down or take a break (*see* Worksheet A14.1 in Appendix 14, 'Fatigue recognition', p80). It may be important to take a break when you start to experience the signs of fatigue identified in Worksheet A14.1. Relaxation may help you to recuperate your energy levels (*see* Appendix 6, 'Guidelines for relaxation').

2. Recognise if you are in a boom–bust cycle

Fatigue can sometimes be maintained by a 'boom–bust' cycle (*see* Figure 4). This means that when you have 'good days' you will do too much and on 'bad days' you will do nothing. This causes problems because of the following.

- If you push yourself too hard, you are likely to have more bad days and thus gradually be able to do less. You will also feel you need to do more on the good days to make up for the bad days.
- If you do too little, this is likely to have a negative impact on your mood, making you feel more sluggish and more tired. This means you will find it difficult to kickstart yourself back into action. Further, if you do not do much, you may also have a tendency to focus on your symptoms of tiredness.
- If you do too little, this will not help you maintain strength and stamina, which in turn will mean that you will tire more easily.

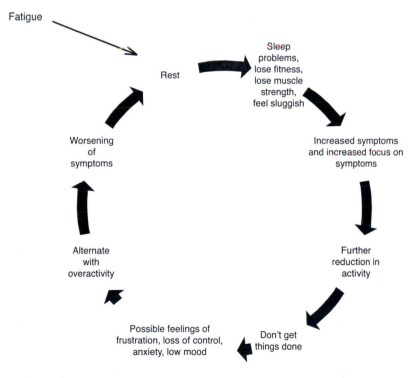

FIGURE 4 Boom–bust cycle

3. Plan your day around your fatigue levels (pace yourself)

To break out of the boom–bust cycle, it can help to plan activity levels around fatigue.

To plan activities around fatigue, you will need to do the following.

1. Write an activity diary and record your fatigue ratings after each activity (*see* Appendix 15, 'Fatigue diary').
2. Use the activity diary to identify:
   - the times of day when your fatigue is at its worst
   - if you are doing too much or too little, which is making you tired
   - if there is anything going on around you at times when you are at your most tired to make your fatigue worse (eg noise, crowds)
   - the types of activities that make you the most tired (eg socialising, physical activity).
3. Plan your day around the scenarios and situations you have identified that make you feel tired; for example, going to the shops when it is less busy. Make sure you take a break after you have engaged in an activity that you know makes you tired.
4. Prioritise tasks that are likely to be important but draining and keep activities to a minimum on those days.
5. Break out of the boom–bust cycle by pacing your activities (*see* Appendix 17, 'Breaking out of the boom–bust cycle: pacing activities', for activity-pacing guidelines).
6. Plan activities and tasks for the times of the day when you have the most energy and make sure you take breaks at the times you feel tired. Alertness is usually at its best between 0800 and 1200, and from 1800 to 2000, although this may vary according to the individual.

Overcoming psychological barriers to fatigue management

- Sometimes people may not want to pace themselves because they believe that they will only get things done if they ignore their tiredness and battle on. It can therefore sometimes be a good idea to review whether this is true and examine the evidence for this belief (*see* Appendix 16, 'Challenging unhelpful beliefs about fatigue').

Other ways to help yourself

- Do not let people put pressure on you to do things you cannot do and delegate tasks.
- Reduce your intake of sugary foods and increase your intake of energising foods such as fruit, vegetables and whole grains.
- Caffeine offers a 'quick fix' for tiredness, but in the long run it makes you more

tired. It can therefore help to gradually cut out all caffeinated drinks (including cof-
fee, tea and cola drinks) over a three-week period. As an experiment, try to stay
off caffeine for a month to see if this helps you to feel less tired. It is possible that
avoiding caffeine will give you headaches. If this happens, try to very gradually
reduce the amount of caffeine that you drink. These recommendations are made
by the Royal College of Psychiatrists: www.rcpsych.ac.uk/healthadvice/problems
disorders/tiredness.aspx.

- Try to keep anxiety and frustration to a minimum (*see* Chapter 3 for understanding
  and managing anger and irritability, and Chapter 4 for understanding and managing
  anxiety).
- Identify any sleep problems and ways to manage them (*see* the next chapter,
  'Understanding and managing sleep problems').

Chapter 6

Understanding and managing
sleep problems

How can a brain injury affect sleep?

After a brain injury, you may suffer from sleep problems because the part of your brain that keeps you alert and manages your body clock may have been damaged. You also may suffer from sleep problems due to other difficulties associated with your brain injury (eg anxiety, low mood and pain). Lack of sleep can make you feel tired, which may affect your ability to complete everyday tasks and activities.

What can I do to help myself sleep?

- Pace your activities. Try not to do too much or too little during the day, as this may affect your stress and fatigue levels and later your ability to sleep (*see* Appendix 17 for guidelines on activity-pacing).
- Avoid sleeping during the day. If you are feeling very tired, try to go to bed earlier in the evening rather than during the day.
- Try to identify what is causing you not to fall asleep. If you are feeling anxious, in pain or depressed, you will need to sort this problem out first.

Establish good sleep hygiene and a bedtime routine by:
- going to bed at about the same time every night and getting up at the same time every morning, even if you have not slept well the night before
- keeping your bedroom slightly warm, not too hot or too cold
- relaxing for at least an hour before going to bed (eg by having a warm bath or watching a TV programme that is not too stimulating) and avoiding doing any strenuous activities
- avoiding caffeine in the evenings
- keeping your bedroom for sleeping only, so that you associate it with sleep
- wearing earplugs if noise keeps you awake.

What if I still cannot sleep?

- Try not to worry about your sleep, as this can make your sleep worse. You will eventually get sleep, as tiredness is like hunger – your body will eventually make sure it gets what it needs by falling asleep.
- Do not worry about what time it is and the fact you are not yet asleep. This will only add to your worry and make it less likely you will go to sleep. Your judgement of time may be distorted, and you may be drifting in and out of sleep without being aware of it.
- Try to relax (*see* Appendix 6 for relaxation exercises).
- If you suffer from racing thoughts, try not to worry about them. Instead, try to detach yourself from them and watch them coming in and out of your mind (*see* Appendix 5 for mindfulness techniques to help detach yourself from your thoughts).
- If you are kept awake by worrying thoughts and things that need to be done the next day, keep a notepad by your bed and jot these tasks and ideas down to look at the next day. Try not to dwell on the thoughts. If you cannot stop thinking about them, try mindfulness exercises (*see* Appendix 5, 'Guidelines for mindfulness').

Sleeping tablets

Monitor the situation for six weeks, and if it seems that your sleep is not improving, discuss this with your general practitioner, who might prescribe you sleeping tablets.

Chapter 7

Understanding and managing **chronic pain**

Why do people experience pain after a brain injury?

People may experience pain after a brain injury (eg if they have damaged their head, face or another part of their body). Brain injuries such as a stroke can also cause damage to the brain that can make even normal touch feel painful. In other cases, pain is felt as a result of muscle tightness or weakness. Pain can often be helped by medication prescribed by your general practitioner, but sometimes the medication may not work. It is important to discuss these issues with your general practitioner.

Sometimes there may not be an obvious physical reason for the pain. This does not mean that the person is lying; there is a psychological component to everyone's experiences of pain. For instance, pain feels worse when our mood is low, when we are tired or if we worry about the pain. A psychological state can have such a profound effect on pain experience that some individuals are able to have surgery without general anaesthetic, just under hypnosis. Similarly, it has been shown that if people view pain more positively (eg a soldier associating his or her pain with the fact that he or she survived a battle and is going home), they are likely to experience less pain.

How does pain affect me?

Chronic pain can be draining and debilitating, causing you to feel low, tired, have sleep problems and may also affect your thinking skills (for help with these problems *see* Chapter 1, 'Understanding and managing low mood'; Chapter 5, 'Understanding and managing fatigue'; Chapter 6, 'Understanding and managing sleep problems', and Chapters 8, 9 and 10 for helping to manage problems with your thinking skills). You are particularly likely to feel low if pain stops you from doing things.

How might I be making my pain worse?

If you experience chronic pain, it is easy to fall into the habit of activity followed by rest, which can make your pain worse. This is called a 'negative activity cycle', as it causes a vicious pain cycle (*see* Figures 5 and 6).

What happens when people become trapped in negative activity cycles?

- If you push yourself too hard, it is likely you will have more days in which your pain is very bad, and you will gradually be able to do less.
- If you do too little, this is likely to have a negative impact on your mood and lower your pain threshold.
- If you do too little, you will also not be maintaining your strength, stamina and flexibility in your muscles, ligaments, joints and bones. A lack of fitness may also make muscles and other tissues tight, meaning that they will tire easily when used or stretched. In the long run, the effect of this is that you will have more pain and feel less like doing any activity.

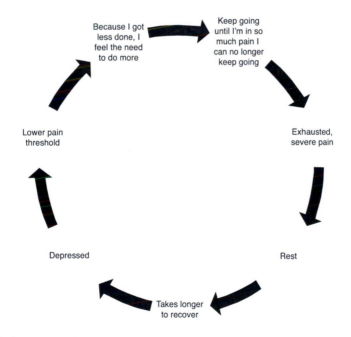

FIGURE 5 Doing too much

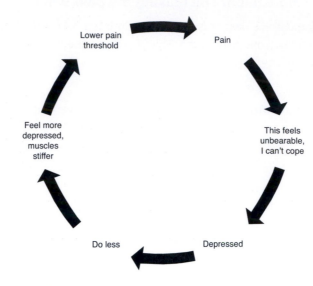

FIGURE 6 Doing too little

How can I pace my activities?

See Appendix 17 for guidelines on activity-pacing.

Relaxation

If your muscles are tense, this can either cause pain or make your existing pain worse. When pain is severe, people normally tense up. It is therefore important to learn to notice when your muscles are becoming tense so that you can relax them. Relaxation may also help you to feel better generally when you are in pain by reducing your anxiety levels and distracting you from the pain (*see* Appendix 6 for relaxation exercises.)

Positive self-statements

It is important to try not to catastrophise the pain. Try to replace the catastrophic thoughts with more helpful thoughts. Some examples are listed in Table 7.1.

TABLE 7.1 Challenging negative thoughts about pain

Catastrophic thought	More helpful thought
My pain will keep getting worse.	No one can predict the future and there are times when it has seemed better. There are strategies to cope with the pain.
The pain will never end.	There is no point in worrying about the future. I just need to cope in the here and now.
My family will leave me because I can't do anything.	There is more evidence that my family loves me and still wants me around than that they want to get rid of me.
The future is hopeless.	There are things that I still enjoy and there are ways in which I can get better. I am coping at the moment despite things being difficult.
I am always sad and in excruciating pain.	I am sometimes sad and in excruciating pain, but this is not always the case.

Mindfulness

People's experiences of pain are also often made worse because they are anticipating bad pain or are worrying about how the pain will affect them in the future. Sometimes, therefore, it can help to accept the pain in the here and now (*see* Appendix 5 for mindfulness exercises).

Useful contacts

Action on Pain
PO Box 134
Shipdham
Norfolk IP25 7XA
Telephone: +44 (0)1362 820750
Helpline: +44 (0)845 603 1593
Website: www.action-on-pain.co.uk
Email: aopisat@btinternet.com

Pain Concern
Unit 1–3
62–66 Newcraighall Road
Fort Kinnaird
Edinburgh
Scotland EH15 3HS
Telephone (Office): +44 (0)131 669 5951
Helpline: +44 (0)300 123 0789
Website: http://painconcern.org.uk
Email: info@painconcern.org.uk

PaIN PUT in Perspective (PPIP)
Telephone: +44 (0)207 188 3236
Website: www.ppip.org.uk
Email: admin@ppip.org.uk

Chapter 8

Understanding and managing
memory problems

How might my memory have been affected by a brain injury?

After a brain injury, a person may have difficulty learning new things or remembering information because of damage to the brain and/or less permanent problems, such as tiredness, pain, low mood and worry, which can all affect the memory.

How can I manage my memory problems?

Day to day, we all have methods we use to help us remember things – for example, making notes or lists. After a brain injury, you may become more reliant on a number of these strategies.

The following is a list of memory problems with strategies that can be used to help you with each.

Not being aware of the day
- Keep a calendar and cross off each day as it passes.
- Make sure that you keep up to date with current events by watching the news and reading newspapers, magazines and checking the internet.

Forgetting appointments
- Write down appointments in a diary or on a calendar and cross off each day at the same time every morning (eg before your breakfast).
- Set an alarm to remind you of each appointment (eg on your mobile phone; *see* 'Useful mobile phone apps' on p33 for reminder apps).
- Put your diary somewhere where it will be readily accessible and easy to find, and keep it with you at all times.

Forgetting things when going out
- Write checklists for what you need to do or buy and tick off or delete each task or item as you complete or purchase it.

Forgetting to do things

- Write notes to yourself and leave them where you will see them. For example, if you have a list of things that need to be done before you leave the house, place this by the front door.
- If you are out and you have remembered that you have to do something, jot this down in a notebook, phone your answerphone and leave yourself a message, or write yourself an email. Some people find it useful to have a memory notebook with them at all times (often electronic notebooks are available on smartphones).
- It may help to get others to remind you to do things.
- Keep a to-do list and look at it on a daily basis. You may want to set yourself reminders (either in your diary or on a mobile phone) to prompt you to review each to-do item just before it needs completing.
- Do things as soon as possible rather than leaving them for later.
- Use electronic prompting devices and services (*see* pp32–3 for websites and mobile phone apps that provide these devices and services).

Forgetting to take medication

- Get into a routine by taking your medication at the same time each day.
- Put your medication by something you already use as part of your morning or evening routine when you have to take medication (eg by your toothbrush).
- Set an alarm (you can buy medication alarm boxes; *see* 'Useful websites and the memory aids they provide' on p32).

Forgetting what people have said

- Leave a notepad by the phone to jot down important messages.
- Keep a notebook with you so that you can write down the key points of conversations immediately after they have occurred.
- If you need to remember information in meetings, use a voice recorder.

Losing things

- Keep important things in the same place and make sure they go back there when you have finished with them.
- Label things so you know where they are.
- Do things as soon as possible rather than leaving them until later.
- Use location tracking devices (*see* 'Useful websites and the memory aids they provide' on p32).
- If you regularly forget where your car is parked, take a photo of where it is on your

mobile phone (eg take a picture of your car and a picture of a road sign where it is parked).

Learning new information

- Make sure you have plenty of time to learn new things.
- Learn small amounts at a time.
- Go over new information again and again until you can remember it.
- Make mental links in your head. For example, if Roger's birthday is on 27 December, you could link his birthday to Christmas (eg think, 'Poor Roger – he'll get joint presents for his birthday and Christmas'). Sometimes incorporating information into a story can help link things up.
- Make visual pictures and make them as bizarre and vivid as possible (eg if your friend's name is Georgie, think of her dressed like Boy George or standing next to him and holding his hand).
- Only try to learn when you are in a quiet place and you are able to concentrate fully. If you feel tired, do not try to learn new things.
- Make sure you take regular breaks. Being tired can make your memory worse.
- If you cannot remember something, try to stay calm and think of strategies or links that will help you remember what you have forgotten; for instance, retracing your steps.

Useful websites and the memory aids they provide

- www.bindependent.com sells a range of alarm watches and other electronic reminders
- http://enablingdevices.com supplies various aids, including vibrating cueing devices
- www.epill.com offers pillbox and electronic reminders
- www.medicalarm.co.uk sells pillboxes and watch alarms
- www.relax-uk.com sells message alarm watches and sleep-tracking watches with alarms
- www.talkingproducts.com offers voice messaging systems
- www.pivotell.co.uk supplies medication reminders
- www.loc8tor.com sells location-tracking devices
- www.alzproducts.co.uk offers reminding devices
- www.tallycounters.co.uk offers tally counters
- www.goconcepts.co.uk/version_2_003.htm supplies automatic spoken in-car reminders
- www.keyringer.com sells location-tracking devices
- www.livingmadeeasy.org.uk offers everyday living devices for severe memory impairment (eg wandering alarms)

- http://brainaid.com/product_v213 sells a range of cognitive aids (Android mobile phone apps)
- http://londonmemoryclinic.com provides on overview of useful websites, resources for memory rehabilitation and self-help leaflets
- www.cogassist.com provides resources for assistive technology

Useful mobile phone apps

Mobile phone apps are constantly being developed and updated. The best way to find a range of up-to-date apps is by typing 'reminders' into the search field of your app store. Some examples of useful apps are given here.

- Alarmed: a mobile phone alarm prompt system that provides a range of alerts, including nagging alerts.
- Sticky Notes: provides sticky notes and reminders on your phone as well as ways to group and organise your notes (eg recipes, holidays and work sections).
- Pillboxie: provides reminders to take medication.
- FutureMe: sends reminders at the time and date of your choice.
- Evernote: puts notes, ideas and images in one place – includes voice reminders.
- Siri (iPhone device): provides reminders that can be set at a particular time or when you arrive at a particular location (eg hold down the home button on your iPhone and say, 'when I get home remind me to take the bins out', and when you get home Siri will remind you).

Chapter 9

Understanding and managing problems with **attention and concentration**

How can a brain injury affect attention and concentration?

It is not uncommon to have problems with attention or concentration after a brain injury. You may have difficulties with:

- concentrating for prolonged periods (eg you may find it difficult to follow a conversation or a TV programme)
- paying attention to more than one thing at a time (eg having a conversation while making a cup of tea)
- ignoring distractions so you can focus on one particular thing (eg ignoring noise going on around you to listen to what someone is saying).

Attention problems can affect your ability to remember and learn new things or cause you to have memory slips (eg forgetting what you went into a room for). They may also affect your ability to carry out everyday tasks (eg cooking or doing the washing). The severity of these problems will vary according to where your brain has been damaged and how severe the damage is. However, the problems may get better or resolve over time.

Strategies

- Sometimes people may find it difficult to do things such as cooking if they find that their attention easily drifts. You can help keep your attention focused by:
  1. breaking the task down into very small manageable steps
  2. writing down each step
  3. following each step in order then ticking each off when it has been achieved (*see* Appendix 1, 'Goal-setting', for a template on which to write steps for planning a goal)
  4. describing what you are doing out loud as you do it.

- Minimise distractions when you are learning something new or when you are trying to do something.
- If you find it difficult to follow a conversation, others can help you out by saying things in short sentences and checking that you have followed what they have said. Or, when there are gaps in the conversation, you can paraphrase what they have said, to check whether you have followed them.
- Try to simplify tasks so that you are only doing one thing at a time. For example, if you are trying to do something, avoid having a conversation at the same time.
- If you find that you have memory slips (eg forgetting what you went into a room for), it may help to keep repeating to yourself in your head what it is that you intend to do until you have done it.
- Do not rush things. Take your time and pace yourself.
- Frequently pause what you are doing and check in with yourself: 'What am I doing?', 'Have I done things correctly?', 'What do I need to do next?'
- It can sometimes help to write an attentional lapse log so you can anticipate attention problems and put in place strategies to manage them (*see* Appendix 18 for an attentional lapse monitoring form).
- Train your mind to pay attention to what is going on around you by reviewing at frequent intervals what your mind is focused on (eg often your mind may be caught up in worries and concerns, which means you will not be paying attention to what you are doing). *See* Appendix 5, 'Guidelines for mindfulness', to help train your mind to focus your attention.
- When you are watching a programme or reading a paragraph, it may help to use the 'PQRST' technique at short time intervals (eg every 10 or 20 minutes, depending on how long you can concentrate before your mind wanders; *see* Appendix 19, 'PQRST guidelines').

Chapter 10

Understanding and managing
executive skills

What are 'executive skills'?

The frontal lobes act as the 'executive director' of the brain. The executive director of a company plans, organises, problem-solves, initiates action, monitors progress and continually modifies plans. To meet his or her target goals, the executive director also needs to communicate with, and get feedback from, all his or her lower-level workers (eg secretaries and marketing department staff). Similarly, the frontal lobes (executive skills) coordinate how we do things, which involves planning, organising, problem-solving, initiating action and so on. They are able to facilitate complex goal-directed actions (eg driving) by coordinating information from other lower-level 'workers' in the brain, such as motor skills, attention, concentration, perception and memory.

After a brain injury, the frontal lobes may be affected, causing problems with executive skills. The extent of the difficulties you encounter will depend on the severity of the injury and where the damage occurred. Any difficulties that you experience may improve over time. Listed here are some things that may be affected by problems with executive functioning and strategies for how you can help yourself.

Kick-starting yourself into action

If you have problems with your executive skills, you may have difficulty getting started on a task. These problems with motivating yourself or beginning tasks can also happen because you are feeling low. If you have difficulties getting started on things, you are likely to have a low activity level, which may have a negative effect on your mood. You can then become trapped in a vicious circle, because the lower you feel, the more difficult you will find it to motivate yourself to do things.

How can I help myself?

- It may help to outline your goals for each week and month and recognise what you need to do to achieve them (*see* Appendix 1, 'Goal-setting').
- Before you start any task, define what it is that you want to do, and define the task

and the steps required. While you are performing the task, check that you are on track and doing what you are supposed to be doing.

- Make sure that every time you reach a goal, there is a reward.
- Timetable activities and tasks for the day and use an alarm system to remind you to do each of them.
- You may have poor motivation, which may not only be related to problems with executive functioning but also be made worse by other factors such as depression (*see* Chapter 1, 'Understanding and managing low mood'), perfectionistic standards (*see* Chapter 4, 'Understanding and managing anxiety') and a tendency to procrastinate (*see* Appendix 3, 'Guidelines for procrastinating').

Planning how to do a task or sequencing an activity

You might find that you are less able to plan or organise how to do things (eg working out a route to travel or organising a birthday party) or sequence a task (eg determining the steps involved in cooking a meal).

How can I help myself?
- Break down the task down into smaller, more manageable chunks.
- Write down, in order, the steps you will need to carry out to complete the task.
- Follow each step in order and cross each off as you complete it (*see* Appendix 1 for guidelines on planning goals).

Solving problems

Solving a problem involves:
1. defining the problem
2. thinking through different solutions
3. monitoring whether your chosen solution is working
4. changing your approach or maintaining your strategy according to what is or is not working.

When you are working out how to solve a problem, make sure you go through each of these steps systematically. *See* Appendix 20 for a problem-solving worksheet.

Contributing appropriately and understanding the main ideas in conversations

If you have problems with your executive skills, you may have difficulty remembering the main points in a conversation, keeping up with what is being said and contributing appropriately.

How can I help myself stick to the point in a conversation?

- Before you say something, think about what the main points of the conversation are.
- Ask the other person to let you know if you go into too much detail or do not stick to the point.
- At regular intervals, check that the other person is following you.

How can I help myself understand what is being said and check my understanding?

- Frequently summarise what the other person has said, to check that you have understood him or her correctly (eg 'So, what you are saying is . . .').
- Ask questions to make sure you do not lose focus and to test that you understand the substance of the conversation.
- Use the 'PQRST' technique (*see* Appendix 19).

Having a realistic awareness of your abilities

You may have an unrealistic awareness of your abilities, or not recognise when you are finding something difficult or making mistakes. This may be because the part of your frontal lobes involved in 'self-monitoring' has been damaged.

How can I help myself?

- Before you do a task, plan it out in checklist form (*see* Appendix 1, 'Goal-setting'). If you complete a step successfully, tick it off; if you do not manage to complete it, try to work out the reasons why you have not been able to.
- Ask a friend or family member what things he or she thinks you may need help with.
- It may be useful to film yourself doing tasks and then watch the film, paying particular attention to the part(s) you struggled with.
- Address any perfectionistic standards or problem-avoiding tendencies you might have. Sometimes self-awareness problems are caused by not being able to psychologically accept perceived weaknesses or failures. This is sometimes caused by perfectionistic standards (*see* Chapter 4, 'Understanding and managing anxiety', and Appendix 10, 'Guidelines for dealing with perfectionism') and a psychological avoidance of accepting that you have problems (*see* Appendix 12, 'Acceptance exercise').

Thinking before acting

You may be more impulsive and find yourself acting before you think. This might be because the parts of the frontal lobes that help you to control your impulses have been damaged. This can sometimes cause people to put themselves in danger (eg running out into the road to greet a friend without checking for traffic first) or be socially inappropriate (eg blurting out something that is hurtful but true because the other person's feelings have not been thought about).

How can I help myself?

- Take your time. Before you do something, stop and think about what risks there might be and the potential consequences.
- Try to pay more attention to how others respond to you. Your impulses are based on your immediate wishes and desires. If you are more self-focused, you are more likely to be impulsive. Thus, it may help to try to pay more attention to your environment and how others are responding to you.
- Ask others to let you know when you are acting impulsively. Sometimes people who are impulsive are not able to recognise this, so it may help to ask others to point this out when it happens and for you to try to pay more attention to the way people are reacting to your behaviours.

Changing your line of thinking

You may find it difficult to change your line of thought, that you obsess more easily or that you repeat yourself.

How can I help myself?

- If you find that you get stuck doing one particular kind of activity, try to make sure there are plenty of things that interest you around (eg books, magazines, the TV).
- If you find that you are obsessing on one topic, let others know and discuss with them how they could let you know when this happens and direct your attention to something else.
- If you have difficulty changing your line of thought because you are worrying about something or frustrated, the thought-challenging guidelines in Appendix 4 may be useful.
- For help changing your line of thinking when trying to solve a problem, *see* Appendix 20, 'Guidelines for problem-solving'.

Chapter 11

Understanding and managing
visual problems

What kinds of visual problems may be caused by a brain injury?

Sometimes after a brain injury, people may have 'hemianopia', which means they have difficulty seeing the left or right half of things. This may be caused by a lesion in the visual pathways (called a 'hemianopia') and/or a difficulty in directing attention towards a particular side of space (called 'neglect').

With hemianopia, usually the individual tends not to see the left or right half of a visual scene (eg a hospital ward), which may cause the individual to bump into things or have difficulty finding things. In contrast, a person with neglect may fail to see the left or right half of a visual scene and/or individual objects or stimuli (eg the individual may only see one half of his or her plate or one half of a word). A person with neglect may also have difficulty focusing attention on sounds presented to and touch on one particular side of their body (although this is not always the case).

A brain injury can also cause other visual problems, such as abnormal eye movements, double vision, difficulties in judging distance and depth, and blurred vision. These problems may be assessed by a multidisciplinary team that includes a neuro-ophthalmologist, a brain injury physician, a clinical psychologist and an occupational therapist. This team should also be able to advise you on whether you need any more specialist support in adapting to your visual problems when you return home (eg whether you need the support of a sensory impairment team). However, visual problems often resolve or improve over time. In particular, if a person has been diagnosed with left neglect (ie he or she has difficulty directing attention to the left half of space), this problem often gets better within the first three months after his or her brain injury.

What can be done to help improve sight of
the left or right half of the world?

- Often, once people have become aware that they are having difficulty seeing the left or right half of the world, they can learn to compensate for their difficulty. It may be helpful if others draw your attention to these problems as and when they occur. Discuss with them how they might draw your attention to these problems in ways that do not make you feel frustrated.

- You can try to make up for your difficulties by rotating your head or trunk to the side you normally fail to see. This has been found to be more effective in people with neglect.
- It may be helpful to aid visual scanning by using your fingers (eg by running a finger along a shelf until you come to the item you are looking for).
- Ask people to approach you from the side you are having difficulty seeing to encourage you to pay more attention to this side. However, if you find this a little distressing, you could ask people to gradually move over to your neglected side at a rate you feel comfortable with.
- If you have trouble eating all of the food on your plate because you can only see half of your plate, once you think you have finished your food, try turning your plate 180 degrees to check. You could draw a line or place a sticker on the plate to mark 180 degrees.
- If you have difficulty reading across a whole line of text, try drawing a red line down the right side of each page and then, when you read, scanning each line until you come to the red marker.

Driving and working

- Visual problems may prevent you from being able to drive safely. As such, if you have these problems, you may need a test from your local mobility centre to determine whether you are safe to drive (*see* Chapter 12, 'Returning to driving'). Similarly, they may impede your ability to return to work (*see* Chapter 13, 'Returning to work' for advice).

Strategies to help you recognise objects

You can help yourself by:
- developing the use of your other senses, such as touch or smell, to help you to recognise an object
- ensuring that the lighting is good when you are trying to recognise an object.

Others might be able to help you by:
- encouraging recognition games, such as giving you objects to name by touch while you keep your eyes shut
- reminding and reassuring you when necessary
- encouraging you to feel and listen to objects that you cannot identify
- being aware that when you are tired, ill or stressed, you may have more difficulty recognising things.

Useful organisations

If you are experiencing visual impairment after brain injury, you may choose to access the services of the Royal National Institute of Blind People (RNIB) and/or The Partially Sighted Society. Both agencies are particularly useful for their talking book and talking newspaper services. The RNIB and the Disabled Living Foundation also provide information about equipment and household items for people with impaired vision (eg liquid level indicators). These organisations may also offer advice on the process and benefits of being registered as partially sighted or blind. The RNIB also offers transcription services.

RNIB
RNIB Headquarters
105 Judd Street
London
WC1H 9NE
RNIB Helpline: 0303 123 9999
Telephone: +44 (0)20 7388 1266
Fax: +44 (0)20 7388 2034
Website: www.rnib.org.uk

Playback Recording Service
Centre for Sensory Impaired
17 Gullane Street
Glasgow
G11 6AH
Scotland
Telephone: +44 (0)141 334 2983
Fax: +44 (0)141 334 2983
Website: www.play-back.com

Playback is a free audio recording service providing newspapers (eg *Sunday Mail*), magazines, a reading service and an audio tape library. Playback will record anything requested by an individual or organisation if it is not available from another source and copyright clearance has been given. The service sends out over 40,000 tapes each month with 20 regular publications.

Low Vision Supplies
176 Belasis Avenue
Billingham
TS23 2EY
Telephone: +44 (0)1642 530801
Website: www.lowvisionsupplies.com

This company produces a range of products that magnifies images (eg books, newspapers).

Disabled Living Foundation
Ground Floor
Landmark House
Hammersmith
Bridge Road
London
W6 9EJ
National helpline: +44 (0)845 130 9177
Telephone: +44 (0)20 7289 6111
Fax: +44 (0)20 7266 2922
Email: info@dlf.org.uk
Website: www.dlf.org.uk

This foundation provides information about disability equipment.

Part 2

Getting back to life

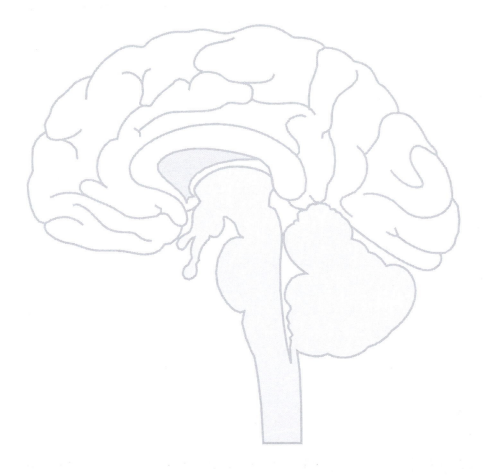

Chapter 12

Returning to driving

Why might driving be a problem following a brain injury?

The Driver and Vehicle Licensing Agency (DVLA) has rules about whether a person can drive following a brain injury. This is because a brain injury can cause problems with a range of skills that are necessary to drive safely, including being able to move, see, concentrate and respond at speed to incoming information. If your skills are impaired in any of these areas, it may be dangerous for you to drive.

What is the process that must be gone through before I can legally drive?

First, you must inform the DVLA if you have had a brain injury, which can affect your fitness to drive. You can consult current guidance from the DVLA for full details of driving regulations (on www.gov.uk/driving-medical-conditions). If there are concerns about your ability to drive, you may be referred to an accredited mobility centre.

What are 'mobility centres'?

Mobility centres assess your ability to drive, which may involve you completing a form and undergoing a physical assessment, a cognitive assessment and an assessment of your driving, usually with a driving instructor. They may also provide assessments for pavement vehicles or scooters, or recommend any adaptations that might need to be made to a car to help you drive. Driving lessons may be available to help you to use a car that has modifications.

Mobility centres also offer advice to help you get back to driving (eg on getting in and out of a vehicle) and can offer help for carers if they need to transport an individual who has difficulty getting in and out of a car. In some cases they may also offer help and advice on overcoming mild anxieties and lack of confidence in relation to driving. However, if you have more significant worries about travelling in a car, it may be important to speak to your general practitioner, who can refer you for psychological therapy.

There is a network of mobility centres covering England, Scotland, Wales and Northern Ireland, and you can attend whichever centre is the most convenient for you.

Further help and advice

The following two organisations may also be able to offer you further support and advice.

Disabled Motoring UK
National Headquarters
Ashwellthorpe
Norwich
Norfolk
NR16 1EX
Telephone: +44 (0)1508 489449
Website: www.disabledmotoring.org

Ford Motability
PO Box 7597
Daventry
Northamptonshire
NN11 1DL
Telephone: +44 (0)8456 040019
Email: mobility@ford.com
Website: www.fordmagic.co.uk

MAGIC provides information about Ford mobility vehicles and the Motability scheme.

Finding your local mobility centre

To find your local mobility centre, call 0800 559 3636 or visit www.mobility-centres.org.uk. You can also contact the Forum of Mobility Centres in writing at:

The Forum of Mobility Centres
c/o Providence Chapel
Warehorne
Ashford
Kent
TN26 2JX

Chapter 13

Returning to work

How might my ability to work be affected following a brain injury?

Your ability to carry out work involves using a range of thinking skills, which can be affected as a result of your brain injury. For example, it is not uncommon to experience difficulties with working out and planning how to do things, remembering information, thinking at speed and concentrating. You may also have more difficulty working if you are in pain, tired, anxious or feeling low, and these can all be common problems following a brain injury. In some cases, there may be practical problems with returning to work, such as poor wheelchair access, or, if your job before your injury was physically demanding, it may be infeasible for you to return to this occupation.

How will I know if I can go back to work?

You may not know if you will find it difficult to return to work until you try it out, because work places a higher demand on your thinking skills, emotional resources and fatigue levels. Further, in some cases, individuals with a brain injury find it difficult to recognise when they are having difficulties, because the part of the brain involved in self-monitoring may be damaged. To help you to see if going back to work is advisable, try:
- slowly and steadily doing things at home that will place a greater demand on your thinking skills (eg DIY, cooking a complicated meal)
- gradually building up your activity levels to check whether your fatigue levels can cope with increased activity
- asking friends and family how they think you are managing on a day-to-day basis
- in some cases, referring yourself or asking to be referred to a neuropsychologist who can assess you for difficulties with thinking, mood, anxiety and tiredness and see whether there are ways that these can be helped.

What support is there to help me get back to work?

- Disability employment advisors (DEAs) can help people who have disabilities get back to work. They give advice and practical support to get you back to work, as well as providing information and support on employment rights and benefits. DEAs can be contacted through Jobcentre Plus (*see* 'Contact information' at the end of this chapter).

- Neuropsychologists and occupational therapists can also help to facilitate a return to work by offering help and strategies to manage difficulties.

What can I do to help myself?

- Speak to your employer to let him or her know about your difficulties and find out ways in which you may be accommodated in the workplace.
- Try to arrange a phased return to work (eg start off with one morning a week and gradually build up the time you spend at work) so that you and your employer can identify any difficulties and find ways to manage them.

What happens if I cannot go back to my previous job?

- A DEA should be able to advise what benefits you can receive.
- You may want to consider whether it is possible to remain at your place of work but reduce your responsibility or take on a different role.

What rights do I have?

The Disability Discrimination Act 2005 states that employers cannot discriminate against employees on the basis of their disability, and employers must make reasonable adjustments to the workplace to enable a return to work (eg providing modified equipment; transferring you to another post; making adjustments to the buildings where you work). Further advice can be obtained from DEAs.

Contact information

Jobcentre Plus

These centres offer access to DEAs who can help with Access to Work grants. These grants can provide you with financial support or equipment to help you with your disability (for more details on Access to Work grants see: www.gov.uk/access-to-work). Your DEA will also provide you with information about benefits.

Telephone: +44 (0)845 6060 234
Textphone: +44 (0)845 6055 255
Website: www.gov.uk/
    contact-jobcentre-plus

Remploy

Remploy is a specialist employment service for people with health conditions and those who face complex barriers to gaining employment. It has links with a number of large employers and can assign you a facilitator to help you settle in.

Head office address:
Remploy Ltd
18c Meridian East
Meridian Business Park
Leicester
LE19 1WZ
Telephone: +44 (0)845 155 2700
Email: info@remploy.co.uk
Website: www.remploy.co.uk

Shaw Trust

Shaw Trust is a national charity that supports disabled and disadvantaged people to prepare for work, find jobs and live more independently.

Shaw Trust Enquiries
Shaw House
Epsom Square
White Horse Business Park
Trowbridge
Wiltshire
BA14 0XJ
Telephone: +44 (0)1225 716300
Website: www.shaw-trust.org.uk

EmployAbility

EmployAbility provides opportunities and support for disabled students and graduates who want to get into work.

EmployAbility
PO Box 64655
London
NW3 9NF
Telephone: +44 (0)7852 764 684
Website: www.employ-ability.org.uk

Part 3

Appendices

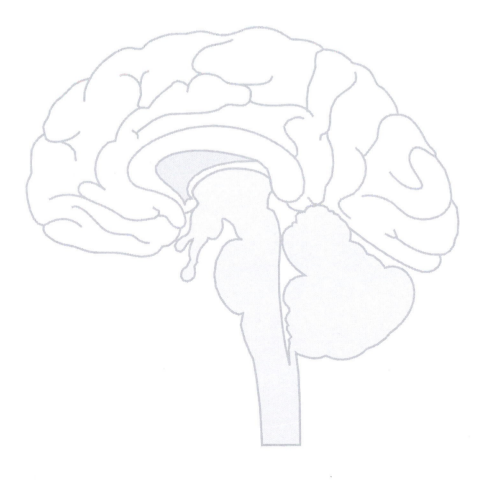

Appendix 1

Goal-setting

Step 1: Set long-term goals

Think about where you would realistically like to be in five years' time in each of the areas of your life listed in Worksheet A1.1.

WORKSHEET A1.1 Long-term goals

Relationships (eg would you like a partner, more social contact, to have a better relationship with your spouse?)
Domestic chores/activities of daily living (eg would you like to be doing more for yourself around the house or to be driving?)
Support and independence (eg would you like to rely less on support from family, friends and/or carers and have more time to yourself? What do you think would be realistic in five years' time?)
Leisure (eg would you like hobbies?)
Occupation (eg would you like to be doing voluntary work or paid employment?)
Education (eg would you like to learn something new or go to college?)

See 'Step 1: Pleasurable activities checklist' in Appendix 2 on p56 for more ideas on goals to set within each of these areas.

Step 2: Make your goals 'SMART'

When you set goals it is helpful to formulate them as SMART goals. These are goals that are Specific (clearly defined), Measurable (you can test it out and see if you have achieved the goal), Achievable and Realistic (only set goals that are achievable) and Timed (you set a deadline for when the goal should be achieved by).

Formulating the goals in this way will help to motivate you, develop a clear plan of action and monitor your progress. Use Worksheet A1.2 below to formulate SMART goals.

WORKSHEET A1.2 Defining SMART goals

Specific	Write down your long-term goal and the steps needed to achieve this (*see* Worksheet A1.3 for how to break down a long-term goal into short-term goals). The short-term goals should include what you need to change for you to achieve your long-term goal (eg are there any problems that you need to overcome to achieve it?). You may also need to think about what resources you may need to achieve your goal as well as any other barriers to achieving your goal.
Measurable	Write down how you will know when you have achieved your goal. This needs to be an observable behaviour (eg what you will be doing differently that will tell you that you have achieved your goal; how will you know when you have completed the task?).
Achievable and Realistic	Check your goals are not too difficult to achieve. To do this, you may need to think about how far away from achieving your goal you are now and what the barriers to achieving it are. You may also want to ask others if they think you are capable of achieving the goal (eg your family or any rehabilitation professionals working with you). If your goal is too difficult to achieve or it is unrealistic, you may want to set yourself an alternative goal. Think about what else you could do that might also provide you with a similar sense of value (eg if you played football with your son before and cannot do this anymore, could you take him to watch the football instead?).
Timed	Set specific dates by which you hope to have achieved the long-term goal and each of the small steps towards it.

Step 3: Create a step-by-step plan for achieving each long-term goal

In Worksheet A1.3 write a description of your goal and then write a step-by-step plan of action for how you will achieve this goal.

WORKSHEET A1.3 Goal-planning

Description of goal:
(eg to cook Sunday dinner, to get back to work or to arrange a party)

Step number	Definition of step	Date by which you hope to have this completed by	Tick when step completed
1			
2			
3			
4			
5			
6			
7			
8			
9			
10			

Appendix 2

Guidelines for increasing the number of pleasurable activities

Step 1: Pleasurable activities checklist

Determine the activities that you enjoy doing using the checklist in Worksheet A2.1. Place a tick next to each of the activities you can do that gives you a sense of mastery and pleasure.

WORKSHEET A2.1 Pleasurable activities checklist

Community and trips		Entertainment		Hobbies	
Going on holiday		Going to the cinema		Playing an instrument	
Going on a trip		Watching TV		Birdwatching	
Going out for dinner		Gambling (eg going to the greyhound races)		Crafts (eg knitting)	
Adventure activity (eg hot-air ballooning, helicopter ride)		Going to the theatre		Photography	
Camping		Going to a sporting event (eg football)		Woodwork	
Shopping		Listening to music		Collecting things	
Other:		Other:		Other:	
Socialising		**Games and sports**		**Domestic activities**	
Speaking to a friend on the phone		Playing on a games console		Cooking	
Meeting someone new		Playing a board game		Cleaning	
Having a discussion with a friend		Playing cards		Doing the laundry	
Visiting family or friends		Horse riding		Gardening	
Joining a club		Playing sports: golf, football, badminton, swimming		Fixing things	
Giving physical affection		Pool or snooker		Baking	
Going out to a coffee shop		Puzzles, crosswords		Taking out rubbish and recycling bins	
Other:		Other:		Other	

Education	Health and appearance	Religious activities	
Learning something new	Buying new clothes	Going to church	
Reading	Putting on make-up	Saying a prayer	
Attending a college course	Getting a haircut	Reading the Bible	
Other:	Getting a beauty treatment (eg nails)	Other:	
	Going to the gym		
	Other:		

Step 2: Plan to do at least one pleasurable activity a day

Write a diary to plan each day or week (*see* Worksheet A2.2). To help ensure that you carry out pleasurable activities within your day, observe the following points.

- Make sure you schedule at least one of the activities you have identified in Worksheet A2.1 every day at a set time. Set your alarm to prompt you to carry it out.
- Do these activities anyway in spite of how you feel! If you have a tendency to put things off, use the guidelines for procrastinating given in Appendix 3 to help you.
- Gradually increase the number of these activities you do over time.

WORKSHEET A2.2 Pleasurable activity daily timetable

Time	Monday	Tuesday	Wednesday	Thursday	Friday	Saturday	Sunday
0600–0800							
0800–1000							
1000–1100							
1100–1200							
1200–1300							
1300–1400							
1400–1500							
1500–1600							
1600–1700							
1700–1800							
1800–1900							
1900–2000							
2000–0000							

Step 3: Pleasurable activity log

Use Worksheet A2.3 to record the day and time you engaged in an activity and how much enjoyment and pleasure it gave you on a scale from 0 to 10 (0 = no pleasure or enjoyment; 10 = maximum pleasure or enjoyment). Also rate how much achievement you felt from doing it (0 = no achievement; 10 = maximum achievement).

WORKSHEET A2.3 Pleasurable activity log

Day, time	Activity	Achievement	Enjoyment
For example: Monday, 29 June, 10.00	Spoke to grandson on the phone	3	8
For example: Tuesday, 30 June, 10.00	Completed 10 minutes of gardening	7	4

Appendix 3

Guidelines for procrastinating

It can sometimes be difficult to motivate yourself to do things because of a tendency to put things off until a later date, or 'procrastinate'. To stop yourself procrastinating: first formulate what you keep putting off as a SMART goal (*see* Worksheet A1.2 on p54); then write down the reasons, or excuses you make to yourself, for putting the task off and the disadvantages of putting the task off.

See the example in Table A3.1.

TABLE A3.1 SMART goal: I will do the housework at 0900 on Tuesday mornings

Reason for putting off task	Disadvantage(s) of putting off task
I am tired and it can be done tomorrow.	I am always tired, so if I always say that I will not do it when I am tired, it will never get done.
I don't like doing it.	Even though I don't like doing it at the time, I feel better once I have done it.
	It makes me feel miserable if things are on top of me and I have lots of outstanding tasks that need to be done.
	Once I get into a routine of doing things, it becomes easier to motivate myself.
	The less I do things, the harder it is to motivate myself.
I am too busy; I will do it another day.	I keep saying this and I never do. If I always say this when I set goals, it will never happen.

WORKSHEET A3.1 Pros and cons of putting off tasks

Write in Worksheet A3.1 your reasons for putting off the task and disadvantages to putting it off.

Reason for putting off task	Disadvantage(s) of putting off task

Then, next time you think about putting off the task, remind yourself of the disadvantages of putting off the task and use them as statements to motivate yourself.

Appendix 4

Guidelines for thought-challenging

Step 1: Identify thoughts

To challenge your thoughts, you will first need to put into words what you were thinking to make you angry, depressed or anxious. This can be difficult for people with a brain injury because they may have problems differentiating a thought from a fact or separating fact from opinion, believing their thoughts to be 100 per cent true (eg 'It is a fact that Jane was ignoring me and I believe this to be 100 per cent true'). This is particularly common with people with a brain injury because they may have problems with abstract concepts (ie recognising something abstract, such as a thought) or shifting their line of thinking (*see* Chapter 10, 'Understanding and managing executive skills'). Sometimes, therefore, it is necessary to try to learn to separate fact from opinion before you can challenge your thoughts. *See* Table A4.1 for how to separate fact from opinion.

TABLE A4.1 Separating fact from opinion

Fact	Opinion
A 'fact' is something that would be considered indisputably true (with 95–100 per cent confidence) in a court of law.	'Opinions' are based on a belief or personal view and are things that you would find hard to prove (you would have less than 95 per cent confidence in them being true) in a court of law.
Facts include: • descriptions of things that you can touch or see (eg a big, red jumper) • actions that describe something that someone is doing but do not tell you about their intention (eg jumping, swimming) • what you can directly hear (eg 'Frank called me an idiot').	Opinions include: • things that you cannot directly see, touch, hear or smell but which you have to infer from what has happened (eg Jimmy has been to the post office for the last two weeks every day, so he will go there tomorrow) • non-physical characteristics about a person (eg Sally is a 'slimeball', Jim is smiling so therefore he is happy) • thoughts about why people have acted in a certain way (eg 'They lied to me')

(*continued*)

Fact	Opinion
	• beliefs about what others are thinking (eg 'Everyone thinks I am a fool because I couldn't get my words out'). These things are opinions because: • if you knew what another person thought or felt, you would be a mind reader • you cannot be 100 per cent sure why a person has acted in a certain way unless that person has told you • you cannot see into the future.

Identifying opinions exercise

To practise separating fact from opinion, try to identify the opinions or thoughts in the following scenarios.

Scenarios

1. I invited Ed round to my house. He went out in my back garden for a cigarette. I asked Ed if he would lock the door behind him. After he had left, I discovered my back door had not been locked. It must have been Ed and he must have done it on purpose.

2. I gave Elliot a letter to post for me. He told me he posted it. It was a very important letter to my friend. The following week, my friend told me that she had not received the letter. Elliot lied to me.

3. Rachel is a house painter. I asked her to paint my house for me, but after she had completed the job, I noticed that some of the painting was a bit uneven. I am not hiring her again because she is a bad painter.

4. I walked down the road and I noticed an old school friend on the other side of the road. She looked straight over at me and then carried on walking. She did it because she doesn't like me and she thinks I am an idiot.

5. Edward is a tall man with dark hair who always seems to be happy. I like him, but he is a bit of an idiot at times.

6. I have organised to get some decorators in to paint my house. They always arrive late. They have no respect for me.

7. Jane has brown hair and blue eyes and she always has a big smile on her face. She is a nurse and is always very kind to people and happy. I like Jane.

Answers

1. Ed left the door unlocked on purpose.
2. Elliot lied to me.
3. Rachel is a bad painter.

4. My friend carried on walking because she does not like me. She thinks I am an idiot.

5. Edward is an idiot who seems to be happy.

6. The decorators have no respect for me.

7. Jane is always very kind to people and happy.

Step 2: Challenge your thoughts

When you are feeling very emotional about an issue your thoughts are often coloured by emotions, which prevents you from seeing things logically (eg if you are depressed you may look at things through your 'gloomy glasses', which skews your perception of things in a negative light; if you are anxious you may see things through glasses that magnify danger or fears). Sometimes, therefore, it is useful to challenge your thoughts in a logical way (*see* the following instructions).

1. The first step to helping you think about things more logically is to identify the thought that is making you feel very emotional (eg anxious, depressed, angry).

2. Once you have identified the thought, ask yourself whether it is evidence based. To do this, first consider how true you believe the thought to be on a scale of 0–100 per cent.

    ▶ On a scale of 0–100 per cent (0 per cent = not at all true; 100 per cent = there is no doubt that it is true), how much do you believe your thought is true? For it to be 100 per cent true there would be no doubt in a court of law that a judge would consider it to be a fact.

    ▶ If you were presenting this evidence in court, on the same 0–100 per cent scale, how convinced do you think a jury would be that your thought is true ?

3. Then weigh up the evidence for and against the thought being true. To do this, think about the following questions.

    ▶ What factual evidence do you have that tells you your thought is true?

    ▶ Do you think it is likely that a judge would consider your evidence sufficient in a court of law?

    ▶ What evidence do you have that your thought is not true?

4. Now try to identify a more helpful thought. To do this:

    ▶ ask yourself what a friend would tell you in this situation

    ▶ ask yourself what would be a more helpful way of looking at things that would make you feel better about yourself

    ▶ ask yourself what advice you would give someone else in this situation.

WORKSHEET A4.1 Thought-challenging form

Use Worksheet A4.1 to challenge your thoughts. First, identify the thought that is making you anxious, depressed or angry. Then, in the next box, identify how much you believe that thought is true on a scale of 0–100 per cent; review the evidence for and against this thought being true and then identify a more helpful thought (use the guidelines outlined earlier in this appendix to help with this exercise).

Thought	How much you believe the thought on a scale of 0–100 per cent	Evidence for the thought	Evidence against the thought	More helpful thought

Appendix 5

Guidelines for mindfulness

Principles of mindfulness

Mindfulness is based on the following principles.

- Often when we are worried or depressed, we worry too much about the past and future and become wrapped up in our thoughts, losing perspective. Mindfulness teaches you to watch your mind and experiences as a passive, non-judgemental observer. This way you learn to gain perspective by watching your experiences with acceptance.

- Mindfulness may include accepting suffering, which is a part of everyone's life and results from a desire to gain control and stability in an uncontrollable and unstable world. The goal of mindfulness is not to escape suffering but to look for happiness while accepting suffering (eg if you suffer from pain or fatigue, it may be important to accept those feelings, rather than trying to fight or ignore them, while carrying on with life in the best way manageable).

- The goal of mindfulness is to accept your present state of being by being focused on the here and now. This is achieved by paying attention to things that you would not normally notice. Mindfulness is all about seeing more of what is around you; taking control of your senses and really taking notice of everything going on. Mindfulness comes with practice, but the more you try it, the easier it becomes and the more things you will notice without trying.

Mindfulness exercises

- Focus on bodily sensations in the here and now (*see* Appendix 6, 'Guidelines for relaxation'). Try to imagine that you have just been regenerated in a new body and are experiencing sensations in this body for the first time. How does it feel, for instance, to breathe, stretch your fingers and toes, and walk?

- When we do everyday tasks, such as walking the dog, we might think about the things we need to do at home or worry. Instead of being stuck in our heads, we could turn the task we are undertaking into a mindfulness exercise. For example, when walking the dog, we could take notice of the sounds around us, what the ground feels like under our feet, the smells and sounds and the tug of the dog on our arm. Similarly, when washing the dishes, we could try to focus our mind on what we are doing by thinking about the temperature of the water, how it feels on the skin, what the bubbles sound like and so on.

- If your mind begins to wander, try to detach yourself from the thoughts by thinking about watching them floating by in a balloon or imagining that you are watching your thoughts appear on a computer screen – you notice your images, sensations or feelings, but you are just observing them and watching what happens and they come and go. You can also bring your attention back by focusing on your breathing.

Appendix 6

Guidelines for relaxation

What is 'relaxation'?

'Relaxation' is a way of letting out pent-up tension. By relaxing, we can help lower our levels of stress, arousal and tiredness. It can help to reduce our adrenaline levels and calm our body down when we experience the following:

- fast breathing
- higher blood pressure
- increased heartbeat
- tense muscles
- sweating.

Relaxation techniques

There are several techniques that you can use to help you relax, including the following.

Quick fix

If you find that you become stressed or tense while you are doing something, here is a quick way of helping you calm down:

1. stop what you are doing
2. pay attention to where you feel tense in your body and try to relax those areas
3. breathe in through your nose and breathe out slowly and deeply through your mouth
4. do this a few times and then resume what you were doing.

Colour breathing

This is a well-known technique that helps calm you down very quickly.

1. Imagine the colour blue, and, as you breathe in, imagine you are breathing in blue calmness.
2. As you breathe out, imagine you are breathing out all of the red tension and replacing it with blue calm. Again, make sure you slowly breathe in through your nose and out through your mouth.

Progressive muscle relaxation

1. Sit or lie down comfortably and close your eyes.
2. Let the tension in your body go as you take some slow, deep breaths (slowly breathe in through your nose and out through your mouth).
3. Take note of how your head feels, especially your forehead and whether there is any tension there, and then release it.
4. Let your whole face relax.
5. Move to your neck and shoulders – let the chair or floor take the weight of your head and let your shoulders and neck relax.
6. Be aware of how your body feels as you let go of the tension.
7. Let your arms and hands sink into the chair or floor.
8. Let go of the tension in your back, and sink down into the chair or floor. Let your hips roll out.
9. Let each breath gradually become deeper and slower; take note of how your stomach is moving.
10. Slowly and gradually work through each part of your body, being aware of whether it feels tense and slowly letting any tension drift out as you allow that part to feel heavier, floppier and more relaxed.
11. Once you have completely relaxed your body, lie still and breath slowly and deeply.
12. When you are ready, slowly count back from 10 and open your eyes. Slowly start to move your hands and feel and stretch your body out. Take a look around the room, and then, when you are ready, slowly get up.

Appendix 7

Anger

Use an anger diary to record times when you get angry. Include the following information:
- direct triggers – what caused you to get angry at that moment in time
- indirect triggers – any things that may have reduced your frustration tolerance, making it more likely that you were going to blow up at that time
- anger intensity – how intense your anger was on a scale of 0–10.

WORKSHEET A7.1 Anger diary

Date	Direct trigger	Indirect trigger	Anger intensity
	What happened to make you angry at that point in time? Who was there? What was said?	What was going on at that time or during the day that would have reduced your frustration tolerance (eg lots of noise, tiredness)?	Circle how angry you were on a scale from 1 to 10 (1 = not at all angry; 10 = the most angry you could possibly be).
			1 2 3 4 5 6 7 8 9 10
			1 2 3 4 5 6 7 8 9 10
			1 2 3 4 5 6 7 8 9 10
			1 2 3 4 5 6 7 8 9 10
			1 2 3 4 5 6 7 8 9 10
			1 2 3 4 5 6 7 8 9 10

Speechmark

Appendix 8

Coping with angry thoughts

Why may I get angry?

Sometimes people get angry because they have angry thoughts about a person and believe 100 per cent that these thoughts are true, which can lead to them not considering alternative explanations for things. This may be partly because they have problems thinking something different once they have their mind set on something (ie difficulty shifting their line of thinking). They also may have problems with abstract thinking (eg separating fact from opinion). These problems are common following a brain injury.

- People may also get angry because other things have recently happened to them to upset them (eg they might have had an argument with their spouse), or they are having to cope with a number of ongoing problems (eg fatigue) so their frustration tolerance is lower (*see* the 'leaky bucket' analogy in Chapter 3).

What to do when I get angry

- To help with angry thoughts, it is useful to be able to separate fact from opinion (*see* Table A4.1 on p60).
  - ▸ 'Opinions' are inner states of mind that include:
    - — thoughts about why people have acted in a certain way
    - — beliefs about what others are thinking
    - — characteristics about a person (eg idiot).
  - ▸ These things are opinions because:
    - — if you knew what another person thought you would be a mind reader
    - — you cannot be 100 per cent sure why a person has acted in a certain way unless that person has told you.
  - ▸ If you get angry, it may help to look at alternative explanations for things (*see* Worksheet A4.1 on p63, and Appendix 4 generally).
  - ▸ You can also check whether there are other things making you angry at the moment (ie ask yourself, What is in my leaky bucket?), which will help you to put your angry thoughts into perspective.
  - ▸ If you get angry, try not to dwell on what has made you angry, because this will just make things worse. It may help to use mindfulness techniques to help you stop dwelling on things (*see* Appendix 5, 'Guidelines for mindfulness').

 69

Appendix 9

Fear-busting

Guidelines for systematic desensitisation

'Systematic desensitisation' is a technique involving you gradually and repeatedly exposing yourself to what you fear in a safe and controlled way. During this exposure process, you learn to ride out the anxiety and the fear until they pass.

Through repeatedly facing your fear in this way, you will begin to realise that the worst will not happen, and you will start to feel more confident and in control.

There are three parts to systematic desensitisation:
1. identifying a fear you want to overcome
2. putting together an 'anxiety hierarchy' to gradually expose yourself to this fear
3. using relaxation techniques when you expose yourself to the things in your hierarchy (*see* Appendix 6 for relaxation techniques).

Anxiety hierarchy

An anxiety hierarchy provides a framework for gradually exposing you to scary situations in a graded way. You can either directly expose yourself to the situation or expose yourself to the situation in your imagination.

Constructing the hierarchy

Use Worksheet A9.1 to create a hierarchy of scary situations.
1. Think of approximately 10 scenarios that each have a different intensity of scariness. Write them down and make sure they are well described. For example, if you want to overcome a fear of crowds, a really scary situation might be having to travel on a very overcrowded train, and a less scary one might be being in a supermarket at off-peak shopping times, or imagining that you are on a bus with only a few people.
2. Give each scenario a score out of 100 according to how scared it makes you feel (0 = not at all scared; 100 = the most scared you could possibly be). This will help to make sure that you have a varied set of scary situations.

3. Place each of the scenarios into one of the following categories according to its score out of 100; try to have at least one situation in each category:
   - ▶ low anxiety   1–19
   - ▶ medium–low anxiety   20–39
   - ▶ medium anxiety   40–59
   - ▶ medium–high anxiety   60–79
   - ▶ high anxiety   80–100.
4. Once you have finished creating your hierarchy, put all of the situations in order to create your anxiety hierarchy for your particular fear, using Worksheet A9.1.

Facing your fears

The next step is to gradually face the fears you have identified in this hierarchy. It can sometimes help you to face your fears if you try to use relaxation techniques while you are exposing yourself to the scary situation. This is because it is not possible for the body to feel anxious and relaxed at the same time. When you expose yourself to your fears do the following.

1. Practise relaxation techniques (*see* Appendix 6) and make sure you can use them effectively. While you are facing your anxieties, make sure you try to relax using these techniques.
2. Expose yourself to each anxiety situation in turn, starting with what is at the bottom of your hierarchy (the easiest to face). Rate your anxiety at the beginning of the exposure (on a scale from 0 to 100).
3. Continue to expose yourself to each particular situation until you start to notice your anxiety is decreasing to a manageable level, or for as long as you can cope with (rate your anxiety on a scale from 0 to 100).
4. Do not move onto the next step in your hierarchy until your anxiety in the situation you have exposed yourself to has reached a manageable level (eg 50 per cent) at the beginning of the exposure time. Keep practising until your anxiety reduces to this level.

As you move up the hierarchy towards the more worrying scenarios, each should be easier to face because you have desensitised yourself to the ones before them. Use Worksheet A9.2 to rate your fears before and after you have exposed yourself to the scary situation.

WORKSHEET A9.1 Anxiety hierarchy

Use Worksheet A9.1 to create your hierarchy of scary situations.

Scary situation	How scary situation is on scale of 0–100 per cent

Use Worksheet A9.2 to monitor your anxiety levels during exposure to the scary situations. At the beginning of the exposure rate your anxiety on a scale of 0–100 per cent and at the end of the exposure rate your anxiety on a scale of 0–100 per cent (0 per cent = not at all anxious; 50 per cent = moderately anxious; 100 per cent = the most scared you could possibly be).

WORKSHEET A9.2 Anxiety ratings for exposure

Scary situation	Anxiety rating at beginning of exposure (scale: 0–100 per cent)	Anxiety at end of exposure (scale: 0–100 per cent)

Appendix 10

Guidelines for dealing with perfectionism

Perfectionism exercise

Often people find it difficult to give up perfectionist standards because they have beliefs about why it is so important to have high standards (eg 'Striving to achieve perfectionist standards has done nothing but make me achieve the best possible outcome for myself throughout my life').

Review whether this is true by examining the evidence that supports the belief 'My perfectionistic standards do not always result in the best outcome' (*see* the examples in Table A10.1). To help with this exercise, think of times when

- you gave up on something because you were so frustrated about not winning or at doing badly at something
- your performance suffered because of your nerves
- you were not happy with yourself because you failed when you set goals that were unachievable
- you did not attempt something or you completed something late because you were so worried about not achieving '110 per cent'
- think about experiences that support this belief throughout your life (before your brain injury, after your brain injury and at different ages).

See the example in Table A10.1.

TABLE A10.1 My perfectionistic standards do not always result in the best outcome

Age	Evidence supporting the belief: 'My perfectionistic standards do not always result in the best outcome'
Generally, before injury	I felt as though I should always achieve better and therefore was not happy with myself and felt inferior.
12–15 years old	At school, I only tried at the things that I was good at because I was worried about not succeeding. This made me underachieve.
16–18 years old	I liked cycling but only in competitions. I often trained so hard that I got injured and then could not compete.
19–25 years old	I used to play golf, and when I did badly I would throw my clubs down. The more frustrated I got, the worse I got.
26–30 years old	I started a college course but I always handed in work late because I was so worried about getting everything right. I also tended to focus on the minutiae when answering questions. I therefore sometimes missed the bigger picture and did not answer questions properly.
>30 years old	I gave speeches at work, and when I first started I was very nervous, which affected my performance. I always needed to look the best and have the best things, and because of this, I got myself thousands of pounds into debt.
After my brain injury	I sometimes set myself goals that are too difficult to achieve, and then when I don't I achieve them, I call myself rude names and get frustrated with myself. I find it hard to praise myself when I achieve smaller goals, which means I am never happy with myself. Sometimes I only try to achieve the highest goals possible and don't try things that I consider too 'low level'.

WORKSHEET A10.1 Template for recording evidence against perfectionistic standards

Age	Record evidence that supports the belief: 'My perfectionistic standards do not always result in the best outcome'
Generally, before injury	
12–15 years old	
16–18 years old	
19–25 years old	
26–30 years old	
>30 years old	
After my brain injury	

Appendix 11

'Good old days' bias exercise

As mentioned in Chapter 4, frequently people view how they were before their brain injury through rose-tinted glasses (eg they think, 'I never made mistakes before my brain injury and my memory was 100 per cent perfect') and view themselves through gloomy glasses after the brain injury (eg 'I always make mistakes now'). This is known as the 'good old days' bias. This can be unhelpful, as it sometimes can cause you to perceive your problems to be much worse that they really are. It also can prevent you from managing aspects of your problems that are not necessarily related to a brain injury.

To challenge this belief do the following.

- Identify what cognitive problems (ie problems with thinking skills such as slow thinking speed, memory slips) and emotional problems (eg anger, anxiety) you have now, how frequently you experience these problems and how bad the problems are (eg what do they stop you from doing or cause you difficulty doing?).
- Then examine how these problems are now, compared with how they were prior to your brain injury.
- Also think about whether there are any other reasons for these differences that are not related to your brain injury (eg if you forget many appointments now, is this partly because you have many more appointments that you did before?). If you identify reasons for these changes that are not due to the brain injury, this does *not* mean that the changes are not related to a brain injury. Often cognitive and emotional changes are due to a range of factors related to both brain injury and non-brain injury.

See the example in Table A11.1.

TABLE A11.1 'Good old days' bias exercise

Experiences of cognitive and emotional problems after brain injury	Experience of these problems before the brain injury	Possible reasons not related to the brain injury that may contribute to differences before and after injury
I have slow speed of thinking all the time but it does not stop me doing anything.	I sometimes had slowed speed of thinking before but only when I was tired.	I am doing too much overtime at work to try to make up for time I have had off. This is making me very tired.
I forget to lock the door twice a month.	I forgot to lock the door before but only approximately twice a year when I was very stressed.	I am much more stressed now.
I get angry with my husband every day and shout at him.	I got angry with my husband before and shouted at him but this was only once a week.	We have financial pressures, and this is causing arguments.
I forget about 50 per cent of my appointments.	I only forgot appointments about once a year before.	I had very few appointments back then.

WORKSHEET A11.1 'Good old days' bias exercise template

Experiences of cognitive and emotional problems after brain injury	Experience of these problems before the brain injury	Possible reasons not related to the brain injury for this difference

Appendix 12

Acceptance exercise

People sometimes avoid setting goals because of a fear of failure or a fear of not getting things exactly right (*see* 'How can I manage my perfectionism?' in Chapter 4, 'Understanding and managing anxiety', p18). In these cases, it may help to set goals that are not focused on doing things to the best possible standard (eg cooking a meal without making any mistakes) but on accepting your problems; feeling comfortable with yourself in the here and now rather than your happiness being dependent on striving for things and achieving perfection.

To set yourself goals for acceptance, follow these guidelines.

1. Set an acceptance goal and formulate it as a SMART goal (*see* Appendix 1). A SMART goal is Specific (clearly defined), Measurable (you can clearly test out and see if you have achieved it), Achievable and Realistic (it is realistic that you will achieve it) and Timed (you set a deadline for when it should be achieved by).

2. Evaluate how successfully you have achieved the goal on a scale of 0–100 per cent (0 per cent = 0 per cent achievement; 100 per cent = 100 per cent successful).

TABLE A12.1 New goals for acceptance exercise

Acceptance goal	Goal formulated as a SMART goal (*see* Appendix 1)	Goal achievement (scale: 0–100 per cent)
Being able to talk to myself with a 'compassionate mind' (*see* Appendix 13, 'Compassionate mind exercise') when I don't get things 100 per cent right	Next time I make a mistake, instead of calling myself a rude name I will say something compassionate to myself (statement identified in Appendix 13).	60
Being able to accept doing things in a simpler way when I need to (eg if I am tired)	Tomorrow I will make a sandwich while sitting on my perching stool.	100
Being able to recognise when I don't do things 100 per cent perfectly (eg my ratings of my performance are the same as my friend's, my family members', my occupational therapist's or my psychologist's).	My therapist's ratings of how many verbal and physical prompts I need when preparing a meal (goal set for next week) will be consistent with mine.	50

(*continued*)

Acceptance goal	Goal formulated as a SMART goal (*see* Appendix 1)	Goal achievement (scale: 0–100 per cent)
Be less concerned about being judged by others (eg mispronounce words when talking to others without becoming anxious)	Tomorrow I will deliberately mispronounce two words when having a conversation with my husband.	100

WORKSHEET A12.1 New goals for acceptance exercise template

Acceptance goal	Goal formulated as a SMART goal	Goal achievement (scale: 0–100 per cent)

Appendix 13

Compassionate mind exercise

How to talk to myself with a compassionate mind

People are frequently a lot kinder to other people when they make mistakes or do not get things exactly right than they are to themselves in the same circumstances (eg they are highly critical and call themselves rude names). When you get angry with yourself for not doing as well as you think you could have, try not to say something harsh and critical about yourself. Instead, try to say or think something kind and accepting – the kind of thing you would say to someone else.

To do this, think about something kind and accepting that you might say to someone who had some of the same problems as you (eg forgetting things, problems expressing yourself). Examples of compassionate mind statements include the following.

- It's OK that I lost my balance getting to the toilet. I made it there anyway, and even though I lost my balance, I did not get annoyed with myself.
- It's OK that I couldn't quite find the right words to explain what I meant; the other person understood me anyway.
- I am admirable for progressing as much as I have while having to accept and deal with my problems. *Remember*: 'Success is to be measured not so much by the position that one has reached in life as by the obstacles which he has overcome' (Booker T Washington).

Use Worksheet A13.1 to identify:
1. the task that is making you frustrated
2. the harsh words you are saying to yourself when you think that you are not doing well ('critical voice')
3. what you could say to yourself instead that is kind ('compassionate mind statement')

WORKSHEET A13.1 Compassionate mind statements

Task that makes me frustrated	What my critical voice says when I get frustrated	Alternative compassionate mind statement

 79

Appendix 14

Fatigue recognition

On Worksheet A14.1, try to note the signs you notice when you get tired. You may want to think about how you think, feel and act differently. It may help if you also get someone else to tell you what he or she notices about you when you get tired.

WORKSHEET A14.1 'Signs of fatigue' monitoring form

Sign of fatigue	Sign present when tired (tick if present)	Time(s) of day when at worst	Time(s) of day when at best
Body feeling heavier			
Mind feeling 'foggy' or 'cloudy'			
Slowed thinking			
Feeling confused			
Forgetting things			
Low motivation			
Anxiety			
Frustration			
Low mood			
Slurred speech			
Any other sign(s) noticed:			

Appendix 15

Fatigue diary

After every hour, record in a fatigue diary (*see* Worksheet A15.1) what you have done in that time (including if you have been sitting doing nothing). Next to each activity in your fatigue diary, give yourself a score on the fatigue rating scale from 0 to 10 (0 = not at all tired; 10 = so tired you need to go to sleep). To help you do this you may want to review the 'signs of fatigue' checklist you completed in Appendix 14. You may want to consider how present each sign on your checklist was on a scale from 0 to 10, so that you can get more accurate ratings of fatigue.

Use your fatigue diary to identify:
- the times of day when your fatigue is at its worst
- if you day is filled with too much or too little activity, which is making you more tired
- if there is anything going on around you at times when you are at your most tired to make your fatigue worse (eg crowds, noise)
- the activities that make you the most tired.

WORKSHEET A15.1 Fatigue diary

	Monday	Tuesday	Wednesday	Thursday	Friday	Saturday	Sunday
Hours slept							
0600–0800							
0800–1000							
1000–1100							
1100–1200							
1200–1300							
1300–1400							
1400–1500							
1500–1600							
1600–1700							
1700–1800							
1800–1900							
1900–2000							
2000–0000							
Time went to sleep							
Hours of activity							

Appendix 16

Challenging unhelpful beliefs about fatigue

People may ignore signs of fatigue because they think that they will achieve a better outcome if they ignore their tiredness and battle on. As such, it can sometimes be useful to challenge whether this belief is true.

Use Worksheet A16.1 to challenge the belief: 'I will achieve a better outcome if I ignore my tiredness and battle on'.

To fill in this worksheet complete the following steps.

1. In the section 'Evidence for belief' list situations in which you achieved more because you ignored your tiredness.

2. In the section 'Evidence against belief' list situations in which you had problems because you ignored you tiredness. To help you identify this evidence think of times both before and after your brain injury when:
   - you have not been able to complete something because you have burned yourself out by not pacing yourself well enough
   - you have made mistakes because you were so tired that you did not stop to take breaks
   - you could not complete everything that you wanted in the day or week because you did not pace yourself and ran out of energy
   - things have taken twice as long because you refused to stop doing something until you had finished it.

Other tips for helping you identify these 'for and against' situations include:
   - review your fatigue diary (Worksheet A15.1)
   - discuss with a family member or professional working with you if he or she is aware of any such situations.

WORKSHEET A16.1 Challenging unhelpful beliefs about fatigue management

Challenging belief: 'I will achieve a better outcome if I ignore my tiredness and battle on'	
Evidence for belief	Evidence against belief

Appendix 17

Breaking out of the boom–bust cycle: pacing activities

General pacing activities

- Write down the advantages and disadvantages of doing too much or too little (depending on what your tendency is). Also identify any barriers to doing too much or too little and how you might overcome these.
- Experiment by making small changes in pacing your activities.
- Write a diary to plan each day or week. Try not to plan too much or too little.
- Put your activities in order of importance and identify the top two or three that either must be done that week or would make you feel better if you did them.
- Plan to do important tasks at times when you are likely to feel less pain or to feel less tired.
- Set yourself regular goals (*see* Appendix 1 for goal-setting guidelines).

If you do too little

- Write a list of things that make you feel better when you do them. Record how much of a sense of achievement and enjoyment you get from doing them (*see* Appendix 2 for guidelines on increasing pleasurable activities). Try to do at least one of these activities per day.
- Try to give yourself a reward once you have done an activity.
- Build up your activity levels gradually over time using the diary plan (*see* the third bullet point in the previous section) and set an alarm to prompt you to start the activity.
- Refer to Appendix 3, 'Guidelines for procrastinating', if you put things off.

If you do too much

- Try not to do too much when you are having a good day.
- If you tend to do too much, think about what you can delegate to others and let others know how they can help.
- Break a task down into small, manageable chunks and take breaks.
- Learn to take a break when you feel pain or fatigue is building up. You may want to regularly monitor your pain levels (eg by rating the intensity of pain out of 10) and then, when it builds up to a certain level (eg 5 out of 10), take time out for a break.
- Make sure you schedule rest times into your day.

Appendix 18

Attention

People can often suffer from attentional lapses following a brain injury. 'Attentional lapses' describe instances when we fail to pay attention to things, which can cause us to forget things. If you become aware of when you are likely to have an attentional lapse, this can help you to either pay more attention in that particular situation or implement compensatory strategies to prevent you from forgetting something. It can therefore help to monitor attentional lapses and think of strategies to help you manage these lapses.

See the example in Table A18.1.

TABLE A18.1 Attentional lapse monitoring form

Date	Attentional lapse	What I could do to manage it
Wednesday, 14 August	Forgot to take the roast out of the oven	Put a timer on
Friday, 16 August	Answered the door and forgot I had something boiling on the hob	Before I leave the kitchen, write down on a piece of paper that I am cooking and keep this in my hand until returning to the kitchen
Tuesday, 3 September	Overflowed the bath because left the room and forgot the taps were running	Don't leave the bathroom until I have finished running a bath – if I do leave the room, throw a towel over my shoulder to remind me
Thursday, 12 September	Forgot to take notice of where the car was parked	Use my phone to take a photo of the car after I park it to remind me where it is

WORKSHEET A18.1 Attentional lapse monitoring form template

Date	Attentional lapse	What I could do to manage it

Appendix 19

PQRST guidelines

Often when we are watching a TV programme or reading something our mind begins to wander. This makes it difficult for us to follow the gist of the information that we are trying to take in. In such instances it can be useful to use the PQRST technique. This is a technique that keeps our minds focused by continually making us review the information with which we are being presented. This technique involves the following steps.

P	**Preview**	To get an overview of what, for example, a TV programme is about, read the summary in the newspaper, or on the internet; or before reading a chapter in a book, go through and read the headings in that chapter.
Q	**Question**	Formulate key questions that you expect to be answered, such as who, when, where and what?
R	**Read/Review**	Read or listen to the material.
S	**Self-recite**	Summarise what you have just heard or read.
T	**Test**	Answer the questions you asked yourself and check that you have got them correct by reviewing the material.

Appendix 20

Guidelines for problem-solving

After a brain injury it is not uncommon to have difficulty solving problems. Solving problems before your brain injury may have come very naturally, without having to think about all the steps involved in how to solve a problem. After a brain injury it is sometimes necessary to break down the steps involved in problem-solving and go though them in a very structured way. Use Worksheet A 20.1 as an example to help carry you through these steps. *See* the following example.

Step 1: Write down the problem

My problem is: *The neighbour is making noise at night, and has been every night for the last month, and I am not getting any sleep. I have asked him politely to be quiet and he has ignored me.*

Step 2: Write down a number of possible solutions (it sometimes helps to search for the problem on the internet to find potential solutions)

Solution 1: *I could go round there and threaten my neighbour with violence.*

Solution 2: *I could make lots of noise myself to annoy him.*

Solution 3: *I could report it to the authorities and get advice from them.*

Step 3: Consider the pros and cons of each solution and how likely you think each one will be to work on a scale of 0–100 per cent (0 per cent = it will not work at all; 100 per cent = you are 100 per cent sure it will work)

	Pros	Cons	Likelihood of working (scale: 0–100 per cent)
Solution 1: *Threaten with violence*	*He might get scared and stop making noise.*	*He could call the police.*	*80*
Solution 2: *Retaliate by making lots of noise myself*	*This may make him think about what he is doing to me.*	*He is likely to retaliate and make even more noise.*	*20*
Solution 3: *Report to the local authorities and get advice from them*	*The local authorities are likely to give me good advice in how to deal with the problem.*	*It may not work and could take a while to get sorted.*	*80*

Step 4: Choose one possible solution that looks as though it may work and which will have the most favourable outcome based on advantages and disadvantages

Report to the local authorities

Step 5: Plan out step by step what you will need to carry out this solution

	Problem: *The neighbour is making noise at night, and has been every night for the last month, and I am not getting any sleep. I have asked him politely to be quiet and he has ignored me.*
Step 1	*Log instances of all noise*
Step 2	*Look on the internet to see how I can report this to the authorities*
Step 3	*Report this to the authorities*

Step 6: Write down how you will know if your solution has worked and a time by which you will evaluate whether it has worked

The neighbour will stop making noise. I will evaluate this in 2 weeks' time.

Step 7: Carry out your plan

Step 8: Evaluate whether it has worked

WORKSHEET A20.1 Problem-solving exercise template

Step 1: Write down the problem

   My problem is:

Step 2: Write down a number of possible solutions (it sometimes helps to search for the problem on the internet to find potential solutions)

   Solution 1:

   Solution 2:

   Solution 3:

Step 3: Consider the pros and cons of each solution and how likely you think each one will be to work on a scale of 0–100 per cent (0 per cent = it will not work at all; 100 per cent = you are 100 per cent sure it will work)

	Pros	Cons	Likelihood of working (scale: 0–100 per cent)
Solution 1:			
Solution 2:			
Solution 3:			

Step 4: Choose one possible solution that looks as though it may work and which will have the most favourable outcome based on advantages and disadvantages

Step 5: Plan out step by step what you will need to carry out this solution

	Problem:
Step 1	
Step 2	
Step 3	

Step 6: Write down how you will know if your solution has worked and a time by which you will evaluate whether it has worked

Step 7: Carry out your plan

Step 8: Evaluate whether it has worked